The Spiritual Guide to

ATTRACTING PROSPERITY

♠

An Hachette UK company
www.hachette.co.uk

First published in Great Britain in 2012 by Godsfield Press,
a division of Octopus Publishing Group Ltd,
Endeavour House, 189 Shaftesbury Avenue, London WC2H 8JY
www.octopusbooks.co.uk

ISBN: 978-1-841-8-1406-3

A CIP catalogue record of this book is available from the British Library.

Printed and bound in China.

1 3 5 7 9 10 8 6 4 2

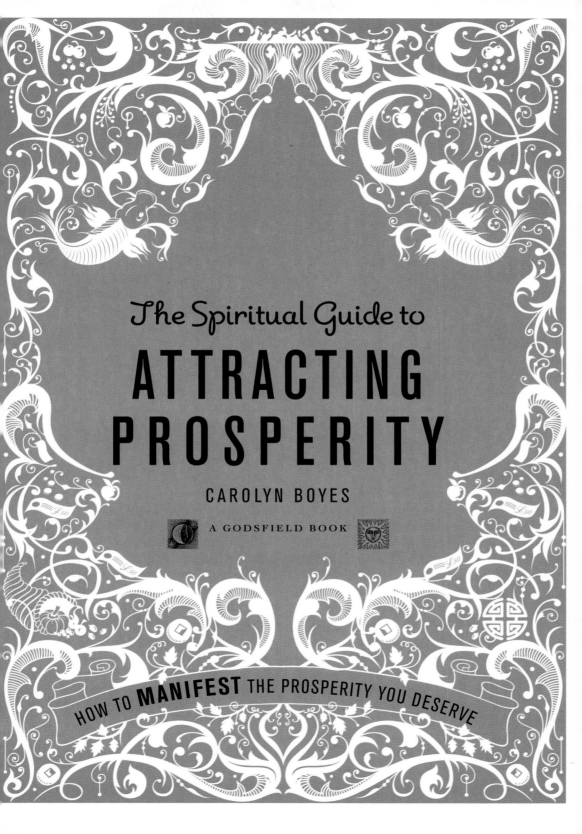

The Spiritual Guide to

ATTRACTING PROSPERITY

CAROLYN BOYES

A GODSFIELD BOOK

HOW TO **MANIFEST** THE PROSPERITY YOU DESERVE

Contents

Introduction

"HAPPINESS DOESN'T DEPEND ON WHAT WE HAVE,
BUT IT DOES DEPEND ON HOW WE FEEL TOWARD
WHAT WE HAVE. WE CAN BE HAPPY WITH LITTLE
AND MISERABLE WITH MUCH."

WILLIAM DEMPSTER HOARD

Do you want to be richer than you are now?

Would you like to be happier and more fulfilled than you are now?
Do you wish to let go of money worries and create the freedom to
do what you want to do with your life?

Most of us want to attract prosperity into our lives and *The Spiritual
Guide to Attracting Prosperity* will show you ways to achieve prosperity
that have worked for people throughout the ages. I will help show
you how to attract prosperity into your own life and also show how
'prosperity' is different from 'money'. You can have a high income or
lots of cash in the bank and still not be prosperous. You can also feel
prosperous with little money when it is used in the right way.

So, does having a particular amount of money equal prosperity?
The answer depends on many factors. What is ample for one person
may not be sufficient for another. The cost of living and average
earnings also vary enormously across the globe, depending on where
you live. How much money you need to buy a home or to feed your
family is not the same in a less well-off country as it is in another, more
affluent society, so you can't be too precise. But whatever the definition
of prosperity, we all share a desire for wealth not for its own sake, but
so we are able to do what we want to make us feel better in our lives.

Creating wealth for the right reasons

This guide will help you to create wealth, but it is only a worthwhile goal when used as a route to attracting real prosperity in your life. It is important to state from the outset that money should never be the end goal, only a means to what you want to achieve by having it. While you need money on a practical level in order to live your daily life, prosperity is the real means to living a happy and fulfilled life. It can be said that you are prosperous when you are able to live a life that makes you happy, meaning that you are happy because you are able to do what you want to do. This also implies your prosperity goes hand in hand with your spiritual wellbeing.

Of course, money is an important part of prosperity, and this book will show you how to create specific goals which, if they match yours, and work alongside and in conjunction with your overall life aspirations, will bring you happiness.

The Spiritual Guide series uses simple but effective techniques to empower you to manifest the changes you want to make in your life. You don't need to believe in or practise a particular religion or faith – the ways of thinking and techniques in this book are suitable whatever your background or culture. The aim of this book is to help you to create a permanent shift in your life. If you truly take this method on board, it will move you from a place where you lack hope and lack what you want, through to the birth of hope and expectation, and on to the realization of your goals.

The information here is taken from a wide range of ancient knowledge and wisdom from around the globe, the primary purpose of which is the following: to change your ways of being in your mind, body and spirit so that you can bring the prosperity you truly want into your life. If you have read other books about principles such as the Law of Attraction, manifestation and creative visualization, or concepts such as goal-setting, or cosmic ordering, and you still haven't yet got what you want, I believe this guide can help you.

Can you be spiritual and rich?

I have experienced both being poor and having money. When I was a child we were poor enough for me to receive free school meals. I made a decision when I was young to change this situation and I did indeed change it in my twenties, subsequently working in the financial sector for 15 years. During this time I was lucky enough to travel around the world, meeting CEOs, politicians and professionals, as well as highly wealthy investors, most of whom were entirely self-made. As soon as I left this world and was no longer sustained by its group belief in prosperity, I came up against the belief that you could not be spiritual *and* wealthy, or even that it was somehow wrong to be spiritual and wealthy.

I disagree with this idea. I don't believe that it is wrong to be prosperous in any circumstance. You don't have to stay poor or to stay feeling poor. If you don't have any money at the moment, you do have the power to change your situation. By taking responsibility for your inner world of thought and the actions you take in the real world, you can attract more money toward you. This guide will help you by providing methods to overcome the belief that you can't combine spirituality and wealth, or that there is something inherently flawed in doing so.

Changing your mindset

This is an abundant world. It's true that some people encounter terrible circumstances in their lives. It's also true that some countries are wealthy and some are poor. Nonetheless, in every situation there is opportunity. More than that though, there are spiritual ways of changing your circumstances. And the principles that apply to a single person are exactly the same as those that apply to a bigger group of people, or even a whole country.

What happens when a country becomes prosperous? Well, of course, concrete action has to be taken. The country sorts out its economy. Perhaps it starts manufacturing things it hasn't made or traded before. At the same time, a change in the mindset of the people within the country has to take place in order for economic progress to happen. In the great economic success stories around the world, people's expectations of how easy it is to attract prosperity can alter. This does not happen only *after* the country has become more successful, but *before* it becomes successful.

FIRST YOU BELIEVE, THEN YOU ACHIEVE – NOT THE OTHER WAY AROUND

This principle applies to you as an individual in the same way as it does to a group of people. Yes, to become prosperous you need to make practical choices when it comes to money and take personal responsibility for your financial success. At the same time, you attract prosperity into your life only if your internal beliefs about the world and about yourself are in alignment with these actions. If we believe unconsciously that it is OK for us to attract something, only then can we attract it. This is because *all* prosperity comes to you because of the Law of Attraction – the ruling principle of the universe that declares that the universe is made of energy and thought, and thought creates our reality.

A prosperous place in the universe

The universe is partly hidden from us. This hidden part of the universe is sometimes called the 'invisible universe', 'spirit universe' or 'unmanifest universe'. The part of the universe we can see and touch is known as the 'world of matter', or 'manifest universe'. The spirit universe contains the source of all creation. It can create, or manifest, anything that can be thought of within the world of matter. If something cannot be thought of, it will not be able to exist.

The universe does not want us to be poor. The universe does not want us to be unhappy. There is a belief out there that material things are somehow morally suspect or that in order to be spiritual you need to retreat from the world and forsake all comforts. There are hermits and monks and other religious followers who live on very little. This is a choice. For everyone else, if you have created little and want to create more, then this is a signal that it is time to take action and change the way you are doing things. It is perfectly possible for you to create a life of prosperity – the universe will support you in doing so.

After more than 20 years of study, I believe that there are tried and tested spiritual attraction methods that work. By reading through the guide and considering each part of the method carefully, you will begin to change your thinking and this alone will help you to manifest more prosperity in your life.

Ultimately, creating change does mean changing habits. First, you need to get to know yourself and understand your thinking habits. You also need to be able to create a clear vision of where you want to get to in your life. Although your vision will involve money, money cannot be the end in itself. You need to know what you want money for and why you want it. Once you have this vision, the universe is able to help you. If you cannot form a clear vision or goal, you may need to deal with some of the limiting beliefs you have about yourself and wealth, or yourself and other aspects of your life before moving forward.

Finally, you need to take action. It is not enough to think about how you can make changes; you also need to follow through. Take action and the universe will reward you. Creating prosperity will come about as a result of actions to change your inner world – your unconscious thoughts and feelings – and by doing things in the real world. Working with spiritual rituals and helpers can help you to reinforce these inner changes and help with your beliefs and vision.

CHAPTER-BY-CHAPTER GUIDE TO THE BOOK

The chapters in this book are best read in chronological order because there is a natural step-by-step way of manifesting a life of abundance and prosperity. After you have finished reading the book and understand the general method, you may want to go back to particular techniques and practise them again. Generally it is a good idea to practise all the techniques more than once. Some rituals, for example those in Chapter 5, are designed for consistent practice.

Chapter 1: Check your thoughts
Learn how the Law of Attraction affects your current levels of prosperity and how to develop maximum prosperity beliefs. Discover that money is just a tool. Learn why your deeply held beliefs can actally attract what you do not want into your life. Learn why lack beliefs will simply attract more lack. Believing you can become prosperous will help you to attract wealth and happiness.

Chapter 2: Find your flow
Learn how feeling gratitude can make you into a natural prosperity attractor. Thank the universe in advance to encourage the freeflow of giving and receiving Tap into abundance – learn how knowing when to give and when to receive creates more prosperity in your life.

Chapter 3: Decide your future
Learn the vital steps that will make a difference in turning your desired future into a reality rather than something you 'want' to happen, but which never does eventuate. You will be introduced to several powerful exercises that you can use to ensure you create prosperity, not just money.

Chapter 4: Play your part
Learn that you and the universe are co-creators of your life. By taking responsibility for your own future you are more likely to make it prosperous.

Chapter 5: Prosperity rituals
Feeling is at the root of all spiritual attraction methods. Learn how age-old rituals
can keep your energetic vibration boosted to its maximum attraction level. You
will be introduced to prosperity props, which you can use to turbocharge your
prosperity intentions.

Chapter 6: Your prosperity helpers
Learn how to choose a spiritual helper you can turn to for support in your quest for
prosperity. Use your creativity to form connections and learn meditation techniques
to communicate with your spiritual guides.

Chapter 7: Daydream your future
Learn creative visualization and active meditation techniques to boost your
manifestation power by removing blocks and activating your dreams.

Chapter 8: Final words
What to do next to make sure your dreams of prosperity really do become a reality.

What to expect from this book

How prosperous can you expect to become as a result of reading *The Spiritual Guide to Attracting Prosperity* and putting its principles into action? Obviously, this book cannot promise that you will necessarily become the wealthiest person on the planet. What is true, however, is that following this method over the long term will create changes in your life that will bring you financial benefit and also create a more fulfilled and happier life. The more you change within, the greater will be the changes without. It is impossible for nothing to happen. As soon as you make any change on the inside, however seemingly small it is, the omnipresent, all-powerful universe will reward you. May you manifest all you desire.

CHAPTER 1

Check your thoughts

'CHANCE FAVOURS ONLY THE PREPARED MIND.'

LOUIS PASTEUR (1822–1895)

Is it time for a change? Do you really desire to have more prosperity in your life as soon as possible? The first step in making any change is to be completely honest about the point from which you are starting. All change happens from the inside out. You need to find out everything you can about why you do not already have what you want. You then need to change your thinking so that you can start to behave differently and attract different people and experiences into your life.

As soon as you make changes on the 'inner plane' – the unconscious world of your thoughts and emotions – you will begin to attract change on the 'outer plane' – your tangible, everyday life.
In this chapter you will learn about:

♣ The Law of Attraction – how your thoughts attracts results

♣ Rich and poor beliefs – which thoughts make you poor and which thoughts make you wealthy

♣ How to change your beliefs and start attracting prosperity by intention, rather than by default.

So what exactly is prosperity?

Let's start with some introductions. Meet some people that I know:

Emma inherited a million when she was about thirty-five. Her grandfather had been a successful businessman and put money into trusts for each of his grandchildren. Emma has always lived her life a bit like a student. She has an apartment that does not have a mortgage on it, but most of the furniture and stuff inside it is second-hand or came from junk shops or flea markets. She has not really changed her way of life since inheriting her money. She works part-time in a juice bar and hangs out with friends. She does not feel financially well-off and worries constantly that she might lose what she gained as easily as she came into it because she does not know whom to trust regarding her investments.

Ryan grew up in a middle-income family. He entered business as a salesperson. At the same time as entering the workforce, he began to invest in property; even when he was not earning a lot of money, he would spend his weekends researching the local property market and made sure that he knew all the surveyors, real estate agents and property developers. He bought one apartment, sold it for a profit, then bought another. When the property market went flat, he successfully applied for a sales job in a small company. He made sure that he was out every night with clients, getting his name known. The next job Ryan went to was not only bigger, but he took his clients with him as well, which meant that he was able to negotiate a great salary and commission deal. Ten years on, he owns five properties and earns a million a year. But Ryan has had a disastrous love life. He has been divorced three times so far. He spent so much time thinking about money that he never made the time to spend with his partner or his family.

Lily is a teacher. She has been teaching off and on for years, and earns a mid-level salary. A few years ago she was offered the chance to invest in an educational supplies company. She decided not to because she did not want to spend her time thinking about business. She also went through a divorce a year ago, but decided not to take money from her ex-husband.

Annette is married to a self-made millionaire. To many people, it may seem that the world is her oyster because she can do anything she likes and go anywhere she wants – without considering the cost. The truth is that Annette's favourite place to shop is the bargain store – one of those places where you can buy almost anything for almost nothing. She does not buy designer clothes or travel around in a flashy car. She is scared of *not* having money one day because she did not do any work to attract it in the first place. On one level she has been very effective in attracting wealth – she is surrounded by it, after all – but on another level Annette is not enjoying the effects of her wealth in any meaningful way.

Rebecca is a successful freelancer in the entertainment world. She commands high fees for her services, even though many other people in the creative fields receive much lower rates. She earns a six-figure annual income, but spends it quickly. She is always the first one to pay for a round of drinks. She loves exotic vacations in far-flung places. She likes to change her whole wardrobe on a six-monthly basis. A year ago Rebecca went bankrupt when the banks refused to let her borrow any more money. She had never bought a home or any permanent asset. Right now she is staying with friends, and she has destroyed her credit card.

I am going to ask you to think about each of these people and to compare their differing situations. This will reveal a lot more about your own views about wealth and prosperity.

ATTITUDES TO MONEY

Do you consider any of the people mentioned on the previous page to be prosperous? Certainly some of them have had money or have had access to huge amounts of money. Some of them have had it handed to them on a plate. Others took every opportunity they could find to make money whenever they were offered it. Personally, though, I would not call any of them particularly prosperous. Prosperity, I suggest, is a state of mind and the following rules apply:

There is no point having money if you have a rotten life.

There is no point having money if you get into debt and the stress causes you to become ill.

There is no point living from paycheque to paycheque if it prevents you from having the freedom to do other things in your life that you would love to do. In the end you will never feel fulfilled.

All these people I have introduced you to control their futures by the ways in which they think – as indeed do you and I. Money is simply a medium, a means you can use to create a particular way of living, not an end in itself. You alone are responsible for taking control of it and creating your own definition of a prosperous life by using wealth wisely, rather than letting it control you.

What do you think Emma, Ryan, Lily, Annette and Rebecca believe about money that has meant they have attracted the particular circumstances of their lives? Obviously only the individuals involved can answer that question precisely, but it is possible to imagine they have differing attitudes toward money and what these might be.

If you have grown up with negative attitudes toward money or you have a lack of financial literacy generally, you will keep attracting a lack of prosperity into your life. This will happen in one of three ways. You will not attract money at all. Or perhaps you will attract money, but spend more than you earn and get into debt. Thirdly, you will attract money, but the very fact of having that money causes the rest of your life to fall apart. For example, you can spend so much time out earning that your marriage falls apart. Alternatively, when you have finally earned the money, you may have become so stressed by the having and the keeping of it that you fall ill.

WHAT IS YOUR DEFINITION OF PROSPERITY?

Take some time to really think about what your definition of prosperity is. For me, having prosperity in my life means that I have enough money to do what I want at the same time as finding fulfilment in work and every other part of my life. Work out exactly what your definition is, deliberately and carefully, otherwise you may manifest buckletloads of money, but end up in a position similar to any of the people I have introduced above. Knowing your definition of prosperity – and you will be asked to think about this in much more detail in subsequent chapters – is the key to creating change. You need to know the end goal of your journey to prosperity before you embark on that journey.

WHAT IS YOUR ATTITUDE TOWARD MONEY NOW?

As well as knowing where you are heading, it is important to know the starting point of your journey to prosperity. Otherwise how are you going to be able to know what needs changing in your current world? You can begin by thinking about your current attitudes toward money.

There are all sorts of people out there in the world with many differing attitudes to money. Some familar examples include the following:

There are those who earn a lot and save a lot, but do not enjoy themselves.

There are those who earn a little, save a lot and have a good time.

There are those who earn well, save for their futures and have a 'rich', full life.

There are those who earn little, spend more than they earn and have fun now, but have nothing put aside for the future.

What is your own individual mindset when it comes to wealth and what would you like it to be like instead?

As you continue reading, allow this question to remain in your mind. Do not worry if you do not have the answers to this or any other questions immediately – your mind will eventually come up with it if you keep your thoughts open and your mind receptive.

THE MIND IS A POWERFUL THING. IF WE REALLY LISTEN, WE WILL ALWAYS GET THE ANSWERS THAT WE NEED.

The Law of Attraction

Why is that some people attract prosperity, while others do not? If you have not already achieved the success you want in your life, then this is an important question. The most general answer has to be that this is because your beliefs about money and prosperity are sabotaging you. And the reason this sabotage occurs is down to the power of the Law of Attraction.

The Law of Attraction is the universal law that governs what we attract into our lives. According to this law, the universe is made up of thought. Thought is energy and we attract into our lives those things that we think about, whether our thoughts are conscious or unconscious. The part of this to really pay attention to is the unconscious part. Your unconscious is a very powerful tool. It is a storehouse for your thoughts and emotions. If you think you want one thing in your life, but you keep attracting the opposite, it may well be that your deep, unconscious beliefs are sabotaging your plans. The thoughts you have are attached to emotions, and a strong thought plus a strong emotion will always and inevitably overrule a weak thought coupled with a weak emotion.

DO YOU ATTRACT INTO YOUR LIFE WHAT YOU WANT?

Is your answer to this question a definite yes? Or do you attract 'accidentally', bringing into your life what you do not want, and repeating the same negative patterns again and again? If you are not attracting the life you want, you have the power to change your life by changing your thoughts and setting out your intention for a new future. For example, imagine that you would like to make money through business but whatever you try fails. You keep attracting failed businesses into your life. You get so far and then the clients stop coming. If this is this case, there may be part of you that doesn't want to succeed or doesn't want to make money. Or, alternatively, perhaps you hold certain beliefs that say you cannot have what you want or you might have a deep-held belief that rich people are nasty. Whenever you start to uncover your deeply held beliefs, unconscious as they may be, you will discover that there are many mixed thoughts and emotions in there, and that these may be at odds with the identity and beliefs that you outwardly project to the world. In the next section we will start to examine your internal beliefs.

Open up your life bag

In the famous Rider Waite Tarot pack, the Fool is the card numbered zero. Have you ever wondered why? It is because this figure represents us at the beginning of our journey through life. The Fool sets out on his journey not really knowing what he will encounter, an act that takes great faith. This is why the Fool is pictured stepping out over the edge of a cliff. (Doesn't it always feel a bit like that when you take your first steps into the unknown?) If you look at the picture closely, you will see that he has a little bit of room in front of him to step forward. The meaning of this is that you always have some room to move and change in your life. In the future, when you look back at the beginning of your journey, you will notice that some of the limitations you thought you had were illusory. You always have the power to move forward.

On his back, the Fool carries a black bag. We all carry baggage with us as we go through life – it is an inevitable part of living. I think the interesting thing is to open up this bag and see what is inside. That is how the Hawaiians think about it. In Hawaiian shamanism, or Huna, it is said that the unconscious mind is like a black bag. Inside this bag are all the beliefs we hold about ourselves, other people and the world in which we live. If these beliefs are negative, they act as blocks to attracting good things into your life. I have always imagined this bag to be exactly like the one on the back of the Fool, with its drawstrings tightly shut, because if the drawstrings are closed then we do not see what lies inside. If our baggage is hidden, we are often unaware of it – which is why it's important for each of us to open up our black bag to examine what is inside.

What is your belief baggage?

Do you know what is inside your baggage of beliefs? Many of us know some of the things that prevent us from making big changes in our lives, but I can also say with certainty that every client I have ever worked with as a coach has been unaware of their deeply held beliefs in their entirety and of how those beliefs affect their attraction patterns. Our deepest-held beliefs – those beliefs that really govern how we live our lives – are often unconscious. They may have been formed long, long ago when we were small children.

Do you think in the same way as other people you know? Do you share many of the same ways of thinking about the world as your family? Or perhaps as part of a wider group? If so, you may not even realize that your way of thinking is just a belief. You may call it a 'fact', rather than think of it as an opinion.

Well, if your beliefs have served you well, that is fine. Do not change what does not need changing. If something is not working in your life, however, take the opportunity to open up that black bag in your unconscious mind – the one like that on the back of the Fool – and shed some light on its contents. Once you have exposed to the light what was previously unknown to you, it can never be concealed again inside the bag. Even if it is supposedly 'out of sight', you will still know it is there. You will now be aware of your thinking patterns, and *that* is the beginning of change.

Are you in 'lack' or in 'abundance'?

The thoughts and beliefs that empower you are 'abundance' beliefs. These ways of thinking allow you to create a flow of wealth and prosperity in your life. They give you more positive choices in life and open up greater opportunities. If you hold abundance beliefs, you feel prosperous and act as a magnet for attracting prosperity into your life.

The thoughts and beliefs that disempower you are 'lack' beliefs. These ways of thinking block you from attracting prosperity and trap you in what is sometimes called 'poverty consciousness'. Essentially this means that, whatever you do, you do not seem to be able to create a feeling of richness and may struggle with debt or just poor money luck. Sometimes people who have a lot of wealth still retain their poverty consciousness and attract either the loss of the wealth or loss in other parts of their lives because of that wealth. Lack beliefs can make you feel poor, or they may make you anxious that you may become poor in future.

Lack beliefs

Here are some common 'lack' beliefs:

Prosperity is just greed.

It is morally wrong to be wealthy.

Poor people are much nicer than rich people.

You can be more spiritual if you are poor than if you are wealthy.

He has more wealth than I so he can't be very nice or certainly not as nice as I am.

Throughout my life, I've met a lot of people who believe that there is something inherently wrong with being wealthy. This belief comes in a variety of forms.

My friend Clari put it something like this: 'I really want to earn more money, but I don't really like rich people. They aren't very nice usually, are they? Poor people are generally much nicer people.'

Lots of little beliefs feed into Clari's statement here. There is the idea that wealth makes you nasty. Clari thinks that not having quite so much money makes you nice and kind, and a better member of society. I am not sure exactly where she got her ideas from, but she is not all that unusual in having them.

For instance, ten-year-old Ellie and I were talking one day, when she said to me: 'I don't want to have money when I grow up because rich people are always horrible.' Now, I know exactly where Ellie got her ideas from: the fairy tales we had been reading. Have you ever noticed how the poor prince or princess is nice in fairy tales, while the rich king is the greedy, nasty person who suffers a horrible fate? These lack beliefs are embedded quite deeply in many cultures. Our beliefs are often formed, like Ellie's, when we are young and impressionable, and come from what we observe as well as what people tell us. We pick up thinking patterns from our peers, our family and our culture, and later we absorb political and ideological beliefs. You don't always need to know where your beliefs come from to change them, but it sometimes gives people a wake-up call when they realize how much they have 'inherited' beliefs from their family, for example, rather than developing them themselves.

INHERITED BELIEFS

Have you inherited any beliefs about prosperity? If so, spend some time thinking about them. Your mother or grandfather or great-grandmother may have had a set of beliefs that was formed during a very different period of history from the one in which you are living. They may well have had far less money than you, or have lived with war or hardship. Do you really want to carry their beliefs through the family line, or would you rather think of new ones for yourself?

GROUP MIND BELIEFS

The 'group mind' is also a very strong influence on our beliefs. Think about how much you were influenced into adopting certain ways of thinking about the world when you were at school. How many of your successes or failures are similar to those of your friends? Have you simply adopted a particular way of thinking that is the same as that of your peer group, profession, culture or country? These are all powerful group mindsets.

THE POWER OF LACK BELIEFS

Lack beliefs do not simply stop you creating wealth in your life or creating happiness with your wealth. They can also sabotage you once you achieve wealth. This is a familiar pattern many self-made millionaires seem to go through. They grow up in poverty, create money, then lose it all again. Why does this happen? It is because they hold conflicting beliefs within themselves at their root level. One part of them really wants wealth and feels that they deserve it, but the other part is thinking, 'I will probably always be poor,' or, 'I don't deserve this wealth, really, because my family have always been poor.'

ENVY

It seems that envy is endemic in our world right now. Television is saturated with programmes, both fictional and non-fictional, showing the lives of very affluent people. Newspapers and magazines are awash with stories of the rich and famous. Some are even devoted solely to the subject of 'celebrity' gossip and accompanying displays of wealth. When I was growing up I thought much more about what I wanted to achieve and what I wanted to be than I did about the lives of wealthy celebrities. It must be tough these days being a child who is constantly exposed to other people's ways of life not to become dissatisfied with your own and jealous of other people who have more than you. But you need to be wary of this type of thinking. Manifesting prosperity founded on comparisons does not work well because it is a form of lack belief. If you are an envious person, you will need to examine your motivations and change your beliefs.

If you look around and say, 'I want to manifest a home like this,' you must have a clear intention to move toward abundance. If, however, you say, 'I want to have more than everyone else because I deserve it more than they do,' your intention to manifest wealth and prosperity is not coming from a place of abundance.

If you say, 'I want what they have got,' but you have envy in your heart as you say it, you are putting out negative energy to the universe. Even if you do create wealth in the short term, those negative thoughts that are attached to your goals are, inevitably, always going to backfire on you in the longer term.

Being powerful

Looking at lack beliefs and underlying negative motivations leads to one belief that concerns power, that it is very important to think about at this point:

Are you OK with being powerful?

It is vital to tackle any mixed beliefs you may have concerning power before going any further. There are many mixed beliefs out there about power — probably because so many people who are powerful in the world have abused their power, not only historically, but also right now all over the globe. Many people who want to be prosperous sabotage themselves once they reach this goal because they are afraid of what other people will think of them for being powerful. A lot of us much prefer to be seen as the underdog and get all of the sympathy that brings from society than to be powerful and face the envy of others.

It is important to be comfortable in all ways with your own power. Any of the changes you make as a result of reading this book are going to give you a lot more power. This can only be considered a good thing because you are going to achieve empowerment, and the ability to help yourself.

A lot of people who believe that they are spiritual do not like to think of themselves as materialistic, and therefore reject power as being too 'unspiritual'. All I can say is, this way of thinking is not going to make you successful in manifesting prosperity. You need to examine your attitude toward your own power very closely before moving forward because, if you have any mixed feelings about it, you are going to get very mixed results in your attempts at creating wealth. Let's not beat about the bush: money is about power in the sense that it gives you the means to do more of what you want in life.

Of course you can always make choices as to what to do with the money when you get it — you then have another kind of power: the power of choice. This is a power that a lot of people around you may not feel that they have, so once again it can attract envy. Creating the kind of magic that is possible with the methods in this book is likely to make you feel different from many people around you. You may feel special or outside the 'normal' way of thinking. You will probably feel that you are privy to power that others do not understand (even though this power is, of course, free to everyone if they are open to it).

HOW READY IS YOUR MINDSET?

If prosperity does not fit with your inner beliefs because they are lack beliefs, you will end up poor again, no matter how large an amount of money comes into your possession. One of the most vivid illustrations of this can be found in the story of the UK pools winner Viv Nicholson. Viv and her husband Keith were living on very little money when they won the football pools in 1961. Keith was a miner in Castleford in Yorkshire.

They won the equivalent of several million UK pounds in today's money. Instead of saving, they spent, spent, spent. Keith was then killed in a car accident, and what was left of the money went. Viv ended up bankrupt, and went through personal and financial struggles over the following years. The transition from scraping a living to exceptional wealth was rapid and she could not hold on to the money. Viv's mindset was not ready.

Abundance beliefs

At the end of the day, what you think about money and prosperity matters only if you are not getting the results you want in life. It seems probable that you are not entirely happy with the amount of prosperity you have in your life or you would not have picked up this book. If so, take a look at the three most common abundance beliefs that follow and read them at the same time as being open-minded about whether they might be true for you.

ANYBODY HAS THE POWER TO CHANGE HIS OR HER LIFE

I was lucky enough to have teachers who really believed in the above statement. As a result, I adopted a belief that, with formal education and self-education, you can learn the things you need to know to make the changes you need to make. All around me when I was growing up there were people who were much richer than me. I could have chosen to believe that meant that I should stay poor. Instead I adopted the belief that I could create a big change in my life. I decided to travel and worked my way around the world. I have been privileged to travel to many different countries and meet the very rich and the very poor.

I have met people who started out with many disadvantages, but who have transformed their lives by making a decision to look out for opportunities. The simple act of deciding to take action to change makes you much more likely to attract prosperity into your life because you have taken personal responsibility for it. Fate alone does not determine our futures. We are co-creators – with the universe – of our lives and are constantly given opportunities to bring ourselves happiness every day.

THERE ARE ALWAYS OPPORTUNITIES TO CREATE WEALTH

I used to invest in stocks and shares for a living. I started this particular career just before the global stock-market crash in 1987 and I learned a valuable lesson. When all around you people think that it is time to sell, there are still always opportunities to make money. This does not mean that you can throw your money around at anything, but it reinforces the idea that prosperity is available to you whatever the economic circumstances – both in a recession as well as in an economic boom.

This has really been brought home to me further over the past few years. I first travelled to China in the early 1980s to learn Mandarin Chinese, when China was opening up to the world and gradually bringing in economic reforms. It was hard for the average Chinese citizen to make money. During the year when I lived in China, the only real businesspeople I saw were fruit and vegetable sellers on the street and the owner of our local eatery. There were very few foreigners there. Shops were nationalized, and we used ration tickets to buy many items such as rice or cotton because the supplies were regulated by the state. A few years later businesses had begun to invest in China, but it was still seen as a risky investment. Now China is the world's great economic success story. World leaders travel there hoping that the Chinese will buy their nations' goods. China has many self-made millionaires and a rich, growing consumer population. When beliefs change across a country about what is possible, an extraordinary metamorphosis can take place. Just think about it. Within the past 20 years, at some point more than a billion people changed their way of thinking – what an amazing world shift has resulted. What would happen if you could change your way of thinking as much as this?

MONEY IS A MEANS, NOT AN END IN ITSELF

How many times have you heard someone make a statement along these lines?

When I am rich I will be happy.
If only I had money my life would be fine.

Do you think like this? Or do you believe that, regardless of how much money you have, you can always make things happen in your life that are positive? People often get confused about money – they think it is an end in itself. Actually, money is just a tool. When you get it, you are still going to have to make decisions about your life. When you are rich, you are exactly the same person – but with money. Some lottery winners who think that their lives will be changed for the better by winning millions are very happy. Some of them spend, spend, spend, and end up no happier than they were before they won. You will attract happiness with money only if you know how to use that money wisely. Identifying money as a tool that you can use to create more prosperity in your life is a very useful way to begin thinking about your beliefs about money. You can then gradually weed out the other, negative beliefs that hold you back and adopt those that are more useful. This will start you on the path to manifesting real prosperity in your life.

First believe that you can make the change, then see it

Closely and honestly examine your thoughts and emotions surrounding the possibility of you manifesting prosperity. Changing your thoughts may seem like an impossible thing to do at first, but it is something you do need to tackle successfully if you are going to make the Law of Attraction work for you and, indeed, if you intend to create any kind of lasting change in your life. I used to think that you had to have evidence that something could happen *before* it happened. Now I know that this is the opposite of how the universe works. Actually, what is true is that you have to *believe* something can happen *before* you see it. You can then begin to create it, and the universe will support you.

All the millionaires I have worked with have this attitude. They have a far-reaching, long-term vision of what they want to achieve, and set out to make it happen. If something goes wrong along the way, they make a few adjustments and keep going.

In Chapter 3 you have the opportunity to decide your future. When you reach this point, think as big as your heart urges you to and do not let your head censor your heart.

We live in an extraordinary world. Think about it. We have amazing opportunities to earn money and we have an amazing freedom to be happy and create the life of our dreams. Travel and technology have both brought incredible changes to the world. Think about internet companies such as Google or Microsoft, IMDB or Lastminute.com. How quickly have they changed our world and the fortunes of those who worked for them? All of these companies contribute to empowering others. And all this happened in the space of less than five years! The world really is speeding up.

Making a permanent change

As you continue reading through the manifestation process described in this book, come back again and again to check your thoughts for any limiting or blocking beliefs. Changing your thoughts for the positive and empowering yourself is the single biggest leverage you have when it comes to manifesting or not manifesting what you want. This is why exercises on changing and mapping your beliefs have been placed right up front here in Chapter 1 of the book. There are also other exercises on changing your beliefs in Chapter 7 (see pages 158–170).

Many people like the idea of manifestation, but think that changing your thoughts is not going to be easy and so they give up. Let's clear up this wrong assumption. At its very simplest, belief change is about using your imagination – if you can imagine your life differently, you can make your life different.

Changing your conscious and unconscious thoughts is all about feeling better. Empowering beliefs allow you to feel happier as a natural consequence because you have more choices about the life that is available to you.

Can you imagine being someone who is happy with a life of abundance?

What would your life be like if you were prosperous?

Whatever thoughts these two questions sparked off, just decide to let them become true. Begin to dream about your new life. Feed your mind with positive thoughts and happy future imaginings, and notice how your mood lifts every day. If you find you need a belief booster, use any of the techniques that follow to help you keep to your dreams. The techniques and rituals in other chapters of the book are also really useful in this regard. There are a lot of different ideas to play with, not because you need to use every single one of them, but because many people find that books with one method only are too simplistic and sometimes do not fit their particular circumstances. A range of choices helps you to tailor both techniques and rituals to what works best for you, so that you can achieve optimum results.

Check and change your beliefs

Let's get some of your beliefs out of the bag. Write down ten things you believe about money:

1

2

3

4

5

6

7

8

9

10

Now write down ten things you believe about prosperity and your ability to create a happy, prosperous life:

1

2

3

4

5

6

7

8

9

10

Identify your beliefs

Identify any beliefs that are lack beliefs. Now really think about these beliefs and challenge them:

- Can you think about any circumstances in which these beliefs might not be true?

- What beliefs would you like to hold instead?

- What sort of person would you be if you changed your beliefs to abundance beliefs?

- What would your life be like?

- Is this something you want?

- If not, what would you like instead? Get clarity and tweak out any inner conflicts you might have.

- What evidence can you find to support these abundance beliefs?

Map your beliefs

A good technique to borrow from neurolinguistic programming (NLP) is to map your beliefs visually on paper. Neurolinguistic programming is very much about self-awareness and changing the patterns of your thoughts and emotions to effect positive results. Write down each belief in turn, then join them together to make a belief tree or flow chart. You can put arrows from one belief to another to show which belief flows out of another belief, or gives rise to more than one thought. By doing this you will begin to see patterns – some beliefs are much deeper than others. If you undo a deeply held belief, you will probably undo several other beliefs at the same time. This is because, when we accept an idea as a fact, we then go through life looking for evidence to support it and adopt other beliefs as a consequence. If you get rid of an inappropriate or limiting deeply held belief, the whole belief 'cluster' will disappear. This is why it is important to hunt out evidence to undo the deepest limiting or blocking beliefs, and indeed to become aware of any unconscious beliefs that may be holding you back.

Draw your belief tree

Draw your belief tree on the biggest piece of paper you can find. Draw in as many branches of your beliefs as you can think of. You will get great satisfaction as you disprove your limiting or lack beliefs and cross out some of the branches or draw in fresh branches with new, empowering beliefs.

You may find it easier to shake up your thinking by drawing two trees to begin with – the first is the limiting belief tree, the second the empowering or abundance belief tree. The second tree does not have to be limited to only the beliefs you have now, but can also include beliefs you would like to take on. Place your belief trees next to each other, so that you can see them side by side. This will get your unconscious really thinking about the benefits of one versus the other. Put the limiting belief tree on the left or below the empowering belief tree. This is because, for many of us, we see the future in our mind's eye as running to the right or in front of us. It is a little trick, but actually works remarkably well to stimulate the unconscious mind.

Now, the Law of Attraction works not just according to our thoughts, but also due to the emotions we have that are connected with these thoughts. If you are clear about which emotions are connected with which particular beliefs on your belief tree, map these as well. You will find that your limiting belief tree contains all sorts of negative emotions. Your empowering belief tree, on the other hand, will contain all sorts of happy and positive emotions. This contrast is a great motivation for the unconscious to make any necessary changes.

Stop to look at each tree and the beliefs (and emotions) that they represent. Really think about one versus the other, and take time to notice how much easier and more pleasant it is to look at the empowering tree versus the limiting tree.

Once you have convinced yourself of the need to change, begin to look for evidence that the empowering beliefs are true (for you as an individual, as well as in general) and that they are the best way forward in your life.

If you need an extra convincer, it is sometimes fun to add to your limiting belief map where these beliefs have come from – family, groups etc. Make the decision to let go of any old family or group patterns, and take on board new beliefs that are suitable for who you are now. Remind yourself that it would be ridiculous, for example, to carry the same way of thinking about the world as a great-grandparent who lived in a different century.

MY BELIEF TREE

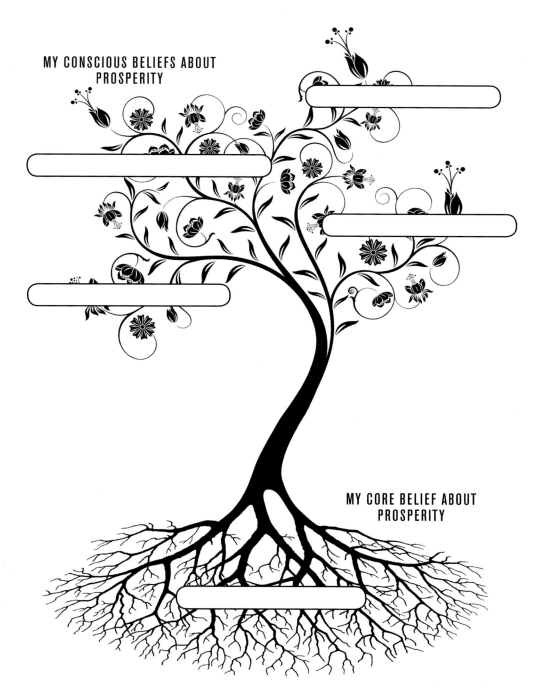

MY CONSCIOUS BELIEFS ABOUT
PROSPERITY

MY CORE BELIEF ABOUT
PROSPERITY

SUMMARY

Thought is the driver of the Law of Attraction. It is vital that you know and understand yourself well enough to be aware of any thoughts, conscious or unconscious, that might block you being able to manifest prosperity.

Take the time to examine your thinking. What mindset have you inherited or taken on throughout your lifetime? Why is it that you are not already where you want to be in terms of prosperity? What are your blocking or limiting beliefs? As you do this, be aware of the emotions triggered by your beliefs.

What evidence can you find for more abundant and enabling beliefs? As you consider this, start to imagine another life – the life of your dreams. Notice how much happier and lighter you feel.

Over the next days, weeks and months, examine and work with your beliefs and find the evidence you need to enable you to manifest your intentions.

As martial arts expert and movie star Bruce Lee is reported to have said, 'I fear not the man who has practised ten thousand kicks once, but I fear the man who has practised one kick ten thousand times.' In other words, keep doing something again and again, and it becomes a habit – a very powerful habit indeed, because it becomes an entirely unconscious skill.

NOTES

CHAPTER 2

Find your flow

'AS A MAN THINKETH IN HIS HEART, SO IS HE.'

PROVERBS 23:7

This chapter is about giving and receiving. Is it better to do one or another to create prosperity? The universe is essentially a world of balance and harmony. To tap into its abundant flow of energy and prosperity, you need to find a balance between giving and receiving, outward flow and inward flow. At the same time, it is important to let the universe know that you are aware of the blessings you already have in your life, so that it is clear exactly what you would like it to help you to manifest in the future.

In this chapter you will learn:

◆ How to be grateful for what you already have

◆ How to tap into the universe's flow of abundance

◆ About the Law of Balance

◆ How to receive and when to give.

A lesson in receiving

When I was about nine, l was offered the chance to be a star at school. I had a good singing voice, and each year we put on some kind of performance for our parents. I had never made it beyond playing a minor-league rat in the *Pied Piper of Hamelin*, so this was my chance to shine. What's more, I knew that I really wanted to be up there singing and acting and entertaining. This was my big break. My teacher came up to me and in a very kind voice asked me if I would like to take a big singing role in the next production. Of course I wanted to. I was smaller and younger than a lot of the other people in my class. This would make me important and popular, wouldn't it? So naturally – or so it seemed to me – I said no.

I did not say no because I did not want the part. I said no because somehow I had got it into my head that it was impolite to say yes straight away to things you wanted. I have no idea where this idea came from. I do not remember anyone ever telling me this, but somehow I associated saying yes immediately with being greedy or arrogant. What I wanted to happen next was for my nice teacher to ask me again and persuade me that I really did want to participate, so that I could graciously accept with my honour intact. Sadly, that was not what happened. Instead my teacher turned to my best friend, and asked her to do it instead. Of course my best friend, having no such hang-ups, said yes immediately – and I went home in tears.

I would like to tell you that I learned from this experience, but unfortunately that was not the case. It has taken me years and years to wake up to the fact that not everyone expects to ask a second time or to press you into accepting their generosity. In fact, sometimes there will be no generosity at all unless you ask. That is a particularly hard pill for me to swallow because, you see, pride comes in at that point. I grew up in poor circumstances, which meant that a lot of our family's time was spent covering up our need, not telling the world about it.

I do not know what your beliefs are about receiving, but I urge you to think about them. You see, the universe will always press your buttons a bit. It is going to bring you prosperity; however, if you need to learn a lesson about prosperity and the way in which to bring it into your life, then it may be that you receive that lesson in the way in which prosperity is offered to you. When I was young I had to learn how to separate other people's generosity from the idea of 'charity'. I had to swallow my pride and not only learn to accept help, but also to do it graciously and with genuine gratitude.

What are your attitudes toward receiving? You may think that you want the universe to give more to you, but are you always happy to receive in the moment? Do you hold any misguided, conflicting or inappropriate beliefs or attitudes about when and how it is right to receive? It would be nice and simple if the universe just handed each one of us a lottery ticket or financial windfall, but that is unlikely to happen. It is much more likely that you will come by wealth in an everyday fashion: through investments, a salary, friends, family gifts or inheritance, or selling a business. Would it matter to you if you inherited money? Would you be OK if you received a gift of a lot of money from a friend or romantic partner?

If you show the universe you are not comfortable with the small gifts it brings – in the form of compliments or opportunities or small gifts of money – it will not give you other, more substantial gifts because you have rejected its generosity. A good place to change any mixed beliefs about receiving is by learning to be grateful for what you already have in your life.

Gratitude every day

How often have you heard the expression 'Count your blessings'? I was brought up in the United Kingdom. I am lucky to have been born in a country that is one of the most affluent in the world and where I have had the freedom to choose the career I want and to move freely to other countries to work as well. I did not have children or a family to constrain me when I was travelling, so I could make the decision to travel to where I thought I would learn the most and earn the most.

Many religious or spiritual rituals, whatever the origin, start by giving thanks to a god or higher being for all that has been provided. 'For what we are about to receive may we be truly grateful' is just one example of this. Many practices also end with words such as 'Thanks be to God' or something similar.

Do you say some form of a blessing before eating? Even if you were not brought up in this way, you can still learn the power of saying thank you. This happened for me when I lived in Japan, where it is traditional to say '*itadakimasu*' (literally, 'I humbly receive') before a meal. No doubt you have encountered or read about similar practices in many households around the world, if not in your own.

Gratitude is an emotion. There have been many studies in psychology on gratitude and its effects. What is clear is that two people who experience exactly the same life circumstances can and will react in very different ways. Imagine that someone in your life has done you a favour. How do you react? The amount of gratitude you feel is not fixed at some standard level. It is determined by the value you put on what you receive, how you perceive the intentions of the person who has given it to you and what you perceive the cost is to the other person. Our interpretation leads us to value or undervalue what we receive.

Why is it important to be grateful for what you already have?

It is very important to feel grateful for everything you receive from other people and for your life in general. It is important to give thanks to the universe because everything you have in your life right now is a gift.

Saying thank you for the things we receive every day is a very powerful process. It reminds us what an abundant world we live in and how generous the universe is toward us. Every time we say thank you for what we have already received, we acknowledge that the universe is there to help us. It has our best interests at heart. Whatever we have now is enough for us in this moment, whether or not we know it at this time.

If you want to create more, all you have to do is to thank God or the universe, whatever you like to call the divine source of all creation, for what has been provided for you already, then ask in addition for what you would like as well. Thanking the universe in advance for what you are about to receive shows your faith in the universe that your wishes will be fulfilled. This keeps you in a prosperity mindset, allowing the Law of Attraction (see page 23) to work for you. It prevents you from falling into lack thinking and poverty consciousness (see page 27).

Start your own daily gratitude habit

Adopt a little ritual of counting your blessings and actually saying thank you out loud once a day. Take a little bit of time out of the day – I find the end of the day works best, but choose the time that feels most right to you. What is key is that you make this a conscious and consistent daily practice.

As you think through what has happened to you over the course of the preceding day, think of at least three things for which you are really grateful. Do not just pay lip service to the universe. Really consider the blessings the day has brought you, even if it has been a tough day at work or at home. Do not discount some of the things you might usually take for granted. You probably still have a roof over your head. Or a bed to sleep in. Or food on the table. Recognize the value of what each second of the day has given you. Even if it has not been an easy day, think about the life lessons you are getting that will really help you later in life.

Now think about how you have helped to bring about each of these blessings and thank God or the universe for supporting you in this by giving you the circumstances and the means by which this has happened. Thank God or the universe for the friends you have around you, your job, the money you earned today, or the space you had to think and dream. There will always be something you can find, no matter your circumstances. In fact, I have met extraordinarily poor people who can always find something for which to give thanks.

As you begin to identify the blessings in your life, you will give yourself the means to attract more and more until your day is filled with blessings. Actually, it already is filled with blessings. You just may not have quite noticed yet. As you begin to imagine your prosperous future (see Chapter 3), remember to be grateful in advance for the joyous creation that the universe is bringing to you.

The Law of Balance

This is a harmonious universe. This is echoed in visual symbols of the world from great spiritual traditions such as Daoism and Tantra, in the yin/yang and the Wheel of Life, where you will see that the universe is always in balance. As already mentioned in the introduction (see page 11), we live in a world of matter that is sometimes called the 'manifest universe' – as opposed to the 'invisible' or 'spirit' universe, which is also called the 'unmanifest universe'. The unmanifest universe is the place of creation. When an idea is seeded as a dot or a spark of creation in the spirit universe, it eventually becomes reality in the manifest universe. It is able to exist in the manifest universe only 'in polarity'. This means that, for it to exist, its opposite must exist as well. For every black there is a white. For every light there is shadow. This way the universe always remains in balance.

The Chinese symbol representing yin and yang shows this beautifully. The two sides of the symbol perfectly balance each other. One is dark and one is light. One is hot and the other cold. In traditional Chinese medicine, both yin and yang 'winds' exist within the body. If you become either too 'hot' or too 'cold', this will manifest as discomfort or illness.

The Tree of Life found in the Western mystery tradition is another illustration of a similar idea. One side of the tree is female. One side of the tree is male. One is dark and one is light. The Tree of Life is a map of all existence. It shows the structure underlying every aspect of the universe. When a spark of creation is born into the world, it moves from the top of the tree down to the bottom of the tree. The path it takes is known as the 'lightning strike'. It zigzags from one side of the tree to the other, not in a straight line, taking on the energies of both sides and keeping perfectly in balance.

This is quite a complex subject, but what it means, put simply, is that the universe likes balance. If we have balance we feel good. If we are unbalanced we have to get back into balance. On a large scale you can see this in the way that economic cycles work. If we all spend too much and go into debt, eventually the cycle corrects itself and we all have to stop spending and start saving to get back into balance. People work in the same way. Sometimes you have up cycles and sometimes you have down cycles. The more you can keep your life in balance, the smoother those cycles will be.

HOW DOES THIS APPLY TO PROSPERITY?

In the natural world many processes are in a state of flux. On a universal scale, by its very definition the universe is never static, but rather in a constant cycle of ebb and flow. Prosperity is no different. If you give, you also need to receive to keep in balance. An abundant universe means that you can let go and give freely, knowing that you will always have enough because you will receive back what you have given and more. Even monks or hermits do this. They may have few or no material possessions, but they agree with the universe that they will give and receive spiritual energy as a counterbalance to their needs being fulfilled. This free flow works automatically as long as your beliefs allow you to both receive and give.

If your beliefs block this flow, your life will not be in balance. Look what happens to misers who hoard their gold. Do they live happily? They may not lose their money, but perhaps their life will suffer in other ways. The classic Dickens tale *A Christmas Carol* illustrates this beautifully. Scrooge was friendless and lonely as a miser until he learned his lesson and gave generously to Tiny Tim's family, immediately opening the door to love and friendship. If you hold on tightly and hoard because you are afraid there is not enough to go around, you stop the flow of abundance and your life will not be prosperous in the true sense because of this imbalance. It was the English philosopher and scientist Francis Bacon (1561–1626) who first said, 'Money is like muck [manure], not good except it be spread.'

How to find your flow

It is very simple. If you wish to receive, you need to give as well. Equally, if you give, you need to receive as well. If you do not pay attention to both giving and receiving, you will inevitably get out of balance. All prosperity is granted to us from the universe. We pay for it in one form or another.

You may wonder why a neighbour or friend has money and you do not. After all, he or she does not appear to be giving to charity or taking care of anybody. Maybe not, but wherever wealth is gained there is some energy exchange going on. Work is one form of energy we give in exchange for money. If you focus on creating wealth – and your beliefs allow it – then money will come your way.

Does having money mean that you need to give it all away to maintain balance? No. Money is only another form of energy. What you do need to do is to think about whether you use that money wisely in the world and how you live your life.

TITHING

In the Judeo-Christian tradition, it has long been understood that it is good to give as well as to receive, and this is how the concept of tithing was born. To 'tithe' means to give away ten percent of what you earn. The word comes from the Old English word *teogatha*, which literally means 'one tenth'. A tithe was historically a voluntary contribution, but also sometimes a tax paid to a religious organization. Tithes in England were not necessarily cash payments, but more often payments 'in kind', such as food offerings. In Europe barns were built across the land to house the agricultural tithe. In traditional Jewish religious practice, tithing has gone on for hundreds of years, with followers of the religion giving away ten percent of their income to charity.

BORROWING WEALTH

Offerings at Chinese temples follow the same principle of giving back. You make a beautiful present of flowers or hard-earned food to the gods, and in return they give you something, be it blessings or good luck. In China and throughout Chinese-influenced Asia, the goddess Guan Yin, the goddess of mercy, is given offerings at her temples in return for her blessings.

Legends say that there were once five hundred guardian angels who wanted to test the extent of Guan Yin's abundance. They disguised themselves as monks and went to her temple to ask for food. The bountiful goddess did not hesitate to give them all food. In gratitude, the angels took some of the food and gave the excess to ordinary people who were hungry because there is always excess available to give. Nowadays, the Chinese go to Guan Yin's temple to ask for blessings, including blessings of wealth. The day to do this is on the 26th day of lunar January, a day that is marked in Chinese calendars as the 'Day of Borrowing Wealth from Guan Yin'. It is seen as borrowing because it is recognized that you should give back something in return for what you receive. If you ask for wealth, you must also be prepared to give something in return, although you do not have to do this the same day. Whether or not you get exactly what you ask for, in Chinese practice, at the end of the lunar year you go back to the temple to return your wealth because a promise is a promise and a contract is a contract. You give something back to the goddess on this day, be it your thanks and prayers or offerings.

CASE STUDY: MEI

My Chinese friend Mei comes from a very poor background. Her family scraped and saved for every penny when she was growing up. Mei studied hard at school and made sure that she received a good training in a profession. She became an accountant. At the same time she put all her spare cash into a dry-cleaning business a friend of hers had started. By the time she was 30, she had saved enough money to buy a small apartment. She continues to work hard and save hard. At the same time as she earns for herself, she also takes care of her relatives and friends, making sure that they, too, benefit from the riches that she has gained.

Not only does this bring Mei great pleasure, but also she believes that in this way she stays in touch with her spiritual beliefs and stops herself from becoming greedy.

The main benefit, though, is a rich sense of belonging to a bigger community. Mei always has friends and family to whom she can turn. They cannot repay her kindness in money or material gifts, but instead pay it back in many other ways, from giving her help with work contacts to helping her with child care, or by simply being there with a friendly cup of tea and a listening ear. 'In my belief system,' Mei says, 'I don't give to receive, but I do think that, if you always help others when you can, there will always be help for you whenever you need it, even if it is not from the same person.'

PUT YOUR MONEY WHERE YOUR MOUTH IS

The idea of giving and receiving as a way of getting into the flow of abundant thinking has already been discussed in the book (see page 55). You can form rituals around giving as a way of cementing your belief in an abundant universe. Using real money really builds your faith and trust, so I would encourage you to make your own rituals of money sacrifice, knowing that this will help the flow of prosperity. Take a look at Chapter 5 (pages 114–135) for suitable rituals you can use.

If you are developing a relationship with a particular god or goddess associated with abundance and prosperity or general luck in life (see Chapter 6, pages 136–157), you can donate money to an organization or temple associated with this particular spiritual power. If not, perhaps you can tithe a percentage of your money to an organization that has associations with the ideas you want to bring into your life. For example, if you are going to use your wealth to help nature, donate to an environmental cause. Businesses that are asking clients to pay for a service will often add a voluntary charitable donation. I do not think that this is the best way to go about things energetically, because it should be you making the sacrifice if you are the business, rather than requiring it of your customers. Instead, decide your fee, then donate to the organization of your choice. Physically handling the cash as you give it away will carry a higher energetic association for you than if you make a credit-card payment. The idea is that it should feel as if you are making a sacrifice, so that you feel the connection to your intention to create prosperity.

Enjoy your money

Just having money piled up in a bank or under the mattress does not build prosperity consciousness. Use your money to give yourself pleasure, and you are telling yourself that you deserve to receive good things by creating a flow of wealth. Enjoy spending your money on the things that make you feel good.

At the same time, stop spending for spending's sake. Some people develop a bit of an addiction to the act of buying. They go out and spend money because the act of buying something makes them feel good, even though they do not really want what they buy. A few minutes later all the pleasure is gone, and they are left with a feeling of guilt, or 'buyer's regret'. Any addiction means that you have an unhealthy relationship with whatever it is that you are addicted to. In the case of spending for spending's sake, you are telling yourself that you will never have enough stuff or that 'enough is never enough'. Give yourself a cooling-off period before buying something, to help you to change your habits. If you can, stop buying anything nonessential for a week or a month, and instead use some of the rituals and exercises found throughout the book to change your relationship with money.

SUMMARY

Take time each day to examine what has happened, and count your blessings. Pick at least three things you are grateful for that day. At the same time, express your thanks to the universe for the positive, prosperous future it is bringing to you – even if it has not arrived in your life quite yet.

Learn to give generously, while at the same time being open to receiving. If you find one or the other easier, practise opening yourself up to the flow of the abundant universe.

As you continue reading through the book, use other techniques and rituals to reinforce your positive abundant thinking. Consider tithing or a similar physical expression of generosity, so that you demonstrate to the universe your faith that wealth and prosperity will continue to flow into your life.

NOTES

CHAPTER 3

Decide your future

'I AM NO BIRD; AND NO NET ENSNARES ME: I AM A
FREE HUMAN BEING WITH AN INDEPENDENT WILL.'

CHARLOTTE BRONTË, *JANE EYRE*

This chapter is all about learning how to create a vision for your future and breaking it down into individual goals. Your decisions will create your prosperous future. In order to create not only money, but also happiness alongside it, it is important to be clear about what you want and why you want it. The 'why' will alert you to what is lacking in your life, while the 'what' clarifies where you will put your focus.

In this chapter you will learn:

- Why money is not the same as prosperity

- How to *see* it – get specific about what you want to attract into your life and define prosperity for yourself

- How to use the breakout technique to undo any remaining blocks

- How to create a prosperity list

- How to *feel* it – make sure you create prosperity, not just money.

Visualize with clarity

The week after I turned 30, I went overseas to earn my fortune. Well, actually, I did not want a fortune, but I did have a very specific amount of money in mind. It was not an arbitrary sum. I came up with this particular amount because it was the general cost of the sort of home in which I visualized myself living. It was far more than I could have afforded to spend up to this point, and so for me it symbolized wealth and prosperity. I had not heard of the Law of Attraction (see page 23), but I did believe that it was possible to create one's own future.

I am not certain that I really knew what I was going to do with the money, but in the back of my mind I felt that this was the amount of money that would liberate me. I would be able to buy a property, then do a job I really wanted to do. Of course I could have just gone to do the job I wanted to do and earned the money that way, but my beliefs at that time did not allow this as a possibility.

I was keen to create this money in my first year on the job. I knew that this was perfectly possible because I worked in the financial markets, with their system of bonuses, plus I was working in a very low tax environment. But at the end of the first year my bonus was smaller than I had hoped. And so I carried on. Focusing on my end goal got me through the next year and a half, when I received a bigger bonus. I still did not have quite as much in savings as I originally envisaged, but I decided to quit my job and return to England anyway. As I was packing up, I received a letter from my employer. While I had been abroad I had paid into some sort of insurance fund. Leaving the country meant that I was entitled to a rebate, and the amount took my total savings to exactly the sum of money I had wanted to create. So, had my goal worked? Well, yes and no. I did end up with exactly the amount of money I had been seeking, but I really had not thought things through in the right way. You see, money really is just a means to an end, not the end in itself. When I arrived back in the United Kingdom, I found exactly the place I wanted to buy, almost identical to the home that had inspired me to begin with, but because I had visualized the money, rather than owning the home outright, what I found was that the cost of property had boomed while I had been away.

The moral of the story – one I have paid attention to ever since – is to visualize what you want to have as the result of money, not just the amount of money that you think you will need to achieve this. In other words, if property prices move as you are in the middle of attracting the money you want in order to buy a property, be sure that your intention to attract the property stands ahead of your intention to attract whatever money you think it will take to buy it.

The Law of Attraction really does work, and it is specific, so you need to be as clear as you can be about what you want. In this chapter you will be asked to think about your dreams for the future and to break them down into individual intentions or goals. (Use of the word 'intention' here is deliberate because it implies that it is something that you have decided to do; the words 'goal' and 'cosmic order' can also be used interchangeably.)

CASE STUDY: BRUCE LEE – THE POWER OF INTENTIONS

One of the most famous stories about attracting wealth is the story of the martial arts genius Bruce Lee. Growing up in Hong Kong, Bruce Lee had a vision of what he wanted to achieve. He was apparently very much influenced by one of the great writers about money and the Law of Attraction, Napoleon Hill, author of *Think and Grow Rich*, which was originally published in 1937. Hill had studied the world's richest men and worked out that they all had a clear way in which they went about attracting wealth – what we now think of as the Law of Attraction method. These wealthy, powerful men all knew exactly the amount of money they wanted to create, with a date attached by when they wanted it. They knew what they would do with it once they had it, and they kept their focus on that sum of money. What's more, each one of them had a plan to get it, even though that plan was, of course, subject to change according to the circumstances encountered. Every wealthy man whom Hill interviewed took action to help their dreams manifest on the material level. They did not just sit there waiting for wealth to hit them; they took definite steps to make things happen, so that they could meet their own deadlines for achieving wealth.

Bruce Lee did become enormously successful, with a big 'but' … When he died it was found that he had written out an exact goal – to achieve world fame by 1970 and by 1980 to have ten million dollars. He had also written of his intention to be the 'highest paid Oriental superstar in the United States'. Did he achieve his goals? Yes in part, but at a price. Fame brought with it its own excesses, including stress, and he died young – in 1973 at the age of 32. From his story we can draw two conclusions. Firstly, that Napoleon Hill's advice works and, secondly, how important it is to make sure that you are truly ready in your beliefs to attract wealth in a happy way, otherwise you will attract money without joy.

The first steps to deciding your future

It is vital to make sure that you are really certain about the future you intend to manifest. So before you think about how much money you want to manifest, think first about your life as a whole. It cannot be stressed enough how crucial it is that you truly understand that it will do you no good at all to create a certain sum of money if you do not know what to do with it, or if you use it in a way that harms you or others. This is why it is important to take the time to think first about what you love doing in life; only after having done this should you consider the amount of money you may need to manifest it.

That being said, considerable personal and professional experimentation has shown me that it can help many people to focus effectively if they also have a specific sum of money in mind that they want to manifest (as long as they are really clear about why this is essential to their other plans). Manifesting money to make other goals happen will help you to build your belief that the Law of Attraction can and does work for you. If, on the other hand, you are already very tuned into your beliefs about your ability to manifest, you may not need this 'means' goal, but instead can simply focus on the end goal – what you are going to use the money for will then come to you. I used to suggest to people that they do this straight away, and indeed this may be the best way for you – that is, form your intention minus the money part – but this does not work for everyone immediately if their beliefs need time and evidence to change.

CASE STUDY: SUE

My friend Sue is entirely trusting. She decides what she wants and she makes it happen. Sue is a counsellor. She spends her life helping others. Her beliefs about manifesting the money she needs are totally empowering. Somehow, exactly the right amount always materializes – she receives a gift of money from a friend, a 'forgotten' sum of money turns up or she receives a legacy. If she is short of money, an extra client appears. She is the perfect example for me of someone who has focused on prosperity, rather than money.

She is so trusting and in the 'flow' of the universe that she manifests incredibly easily. If you would like to be like Sue, or need to spend some time thinking through a clear vision, then a good place to start is with complete and open trust.

What do you love doing?

Prosperity is about using money to create a better life – a life in which you can do what you love to do.

What are you passionate about?

What do you long to free yourself up to do?

One of the reasons that Sue (see left) is so successful in manifesting money is that she loves her work. For her this satisfaction is due to the fact she loves helping people. It gives her great joy to see how their lives change. Of course this is a very appealing career for many people, but I have also had colleagues who are passionate about careers I have no interest in personally. My choices are not going to be your choices. It is really important that you are true to yourself and your vision comes from you rather than from outside influences, because it is only you who will live your life.

Think about the hobbies and interests you have. Are you a passionate quilt-maker who wants to travel the world to study quiltmaking, or do you want to create a life where you free up time every night to go dancing? Perhaps looking after children or animals makes you happy. Perhaps you would be happiest running your own international business or becoming a top lawyer. The following exercise will help you to work out both the what and the why of what makes you happy.

Take the time to jot down some of the things that make you happy – and remember to make this list all about you and not about other people's or society's expectations.

WHAT?

What do you really enjoy doing with your life? What do you want to create the freedom to do? These are such simple questions to ask, but so vital to any kind of intention work. Write down as much as possible.

WHY?

Look at what you have written. Next to each response write down some reasons why this particular thing is so important for you to have in your life. If you decide that it is a 'nice-to-have' rather than a 'must-have', ask yourself the hard questions about whether you feel passionate enough about it to manifest it in your life. Think about what having this will add to your life. What positive feelings will it bring you? What will you need to do to create a balance in your life? What will make you feel good? Are there any activities here that you could use as a source of income?

Next, check the following. If you had all this, would you feel passionate about your life? Anything missing? What are the highest priorities? Are there some that would bring more joy to your life than others?

The key is to get really clear and to think through what a prosperous list would look like and feel like. One of the ways to test that you are on the right track is to sit back and look at what you have written. How does it make you feel? If you experience an excited or happy feeling rising in your body, you are definitely on the right track.

WHY IS WHY IMPORTANT?

Experience shows me that every time I have truly needed money for a purpose that is central either to my survival or my general wellbeing or life purpose, the money has appeared, whether in the form of a banknote on the pavement or in the guise of a sudden gift of work from a client. Create the need for money, rather than making it an end in itself, and money will come to you.

Know why you want the money, and what you are going to use it for immediately or in the long term. There is no point pretending to yourself that you are going to use it to start a charity for empoverished children if you actually want it to buy yourself a flashy car and lots of jewellery. The universe does not work as your moral compass in this way. It is not going to discriminate against you for wanting to have nice things in your life. The only dreams that backfire on us are ones that are not fully thought through. If you want a flashy car and jewellery, then think about how the rest of your life will change as a result. Think about how this will impact others. Think about what kind of person you will become as a result. The same applies if you want money to help empoverished children. It may look like the more virtuous goal on the surface, but who knows what lives you may touch in positive ways by chasing a more material dream? Many of the richest people on the planet end up accidentally or on purpose helping many, many people along the way.

(By the way, if you take issue with the last statement, as I probably did once upon a time, then it is worth thinking about whether you have any negative beliefs about wealth being somehow immoral.)

Make a prosperity list

Start to break down your vision into specific intentions by creating a prosperity list out of your initial brainstorm (see pages 38–43). Think about the life you intend to live, and break down your desires into a bigger list. Expand each entry as much as possible, embellishing the details and being more specific with your 'wants'.

As an example, below is a basic starting list that Tania compiled to get her creative juices going. She then expanded this considerably because she began to let herself dream that she could have all the things that were lacking in her life at that moment.

EXAMPLE: TANIA'S INITIAL PROSPERITY LIST

For me, having a life of prosperity means:

- Paying all my bills with money to spare every month.

- Going on holiday and travelling business class.

- Owning my own home, which I live in with my family.

- Eating out three times a week.

- Being able to pay for gifts for my husband and children.

- Having a new car – it is a silver Mini.

- Knowing I have a great retirement plan and that I can have a luxurious retirement.

- Having enough savings to pay for my children's education outright, while still keeping plenty of savings to afford the way of life I enjoy at present.

♣ Shopping at Harrods in London and buying designer clothes, so that I always look polished in my job.

♣ Buying ten or more friends a delicious meal with Champagne at a top restaurant for Christmas, so that we can celebrate and feel good about the year.

♣ Making generous cash donations to charity.

♣ Treating myself to top gyms, massages, a personal trainer, a secretary, an agent, a top dance class.

♣ Having my whole home renovated and redecorated.

Have a go and get some starting thoughts about WHAT you want by making your own prosperity list.

MY PROSPERITY LIST

For me, having a life of prosperity means:

1

2

3

4

5

6

7

8

9

10

WHY THIS INTENTION IS IMPORTANT TO ME – EXPANDED PROSPERITY LIST

1

2

3

4

5

6

7

8

9

10

The two traps – wants and don't wants

WHY *NOT* WANTING SOMETHING BRINGS IT TO YOU

Here is a trap many of us fall into. Instead of spending our time thinking about how to create a particular future we *do* want, we spend our time contemplating how we are going to avoid all those things we do *not* want.

If you are not feeling particularly happy or if you have a chequered history when it comes to money, this is an especially easy trap to fall into. How many times do you catch yourself doing the 'don't wants'?

Here are a few common ones:

I don't want to be poor.

I don't want to be stuck in a job I hate because I need to earn enough money to pay the bills.

My goal is to make sure that I am never in debt again and never unhappy again or lonely, or anything else I don't want.

The universe gets a picture from you of a poor, unhappy person and probably gets a burst of strong emotion attached to it as well. The thought form is so strong that the universe receives the image loud and clear. Being a perfectly responsive universe, it does its best to create the intention it has seen and felt for you. The result is, yes, you do create more being in debt, being unhappy and lonely and everything else bundled in.

When you catch yourself expressing a 'don't want', think about how you could turn it into a 'want' statement instead. For example:

I want to be rich.

I want to have a fulfilling job that I love where I always have enough money to pay the bills.

My goal is to make sure I always have money and am happy and surrounded by friends every day.

TURN YOUR 'WANTS' TO 'WHENS'

One of the common mistakes that people make is to think that if they want something enough it will happen. Well, you know what? I would like to be in the next big Hollywood movie, but it is not going to happen, partly because I do not believe it is, but also because I have not made it into a 'when'.

Having something you want to happen in your life is very different from having the intention that it will happen. A want can stay as a want. As the White Queen says to Alice in *Through the Looking Glass*: 'The rule is, jam tomorrow and jam yesterday, but never jam today.' A want keeps your future in the 'jam tomorrow' category and never lets you eat it today. To make it jam today, see it and feel it as if it is in your present, happening to you. The universe feels it, too, and begins to create it for you.

Your prosperity list is a starting point (see page 74). It gets what you want out into the open. You still need to take another step after this, which is to turn these wants into goals or clearly stated intentions in your mind (or, even better, into real hard copy on paper or on the computer).

Blocks to brainstorming

Is your past the prison warden of your future? If you look at a person's past, you will find many clues about their future. This was said to me once, and I really did not want to believe it. Are we really victims of our past? Well, the conclusion that I have come to is that you can be, but you do not have to be. Many people do find it difficult to decide their futures for themselves because of their beliefs, including a belief that they do not have the 'right' to change. If you have any lack beliefs (see pages 27 and 28) left from the past, your future is going to be highly predictable: It will be a continuation of your past.

Some people find it easy to dream of a different future. Others cannot come up with anything very much. The latter type of person will say, 'I cannot see anything.' It is true. They cannot see any pictures of their future because their unconscious thoughts remain so focused still on lack and poverty beliefs (see pages 27 and 28). When the reason this is happening is examined, it always turns out that there is a mental/emotional block of some kind. This may have resulted from a past experience that has fed an unconscious belief that it is not OK to create a future of their dreams. It sometimes has come from a group or society belief about it not being OK for anyone to have a prosperous future or earn money and enjoy earning it.

Lack beliefs really are deeply ingrained in many of our lives. It is not surprising, really, when you consider how many wars and famines and other difficult circumstances humanity has been through over the centuries. This group 'thought form' is still present unconsciously in many families because of family history. In addition, if you have been doing a job you have really hated for a long time, you may not find it easy to separate yourself from the 'you' who is unhappy and in that career now. You need to be able to step away from your dissatisfied self enough to believe in different possibilities for your future.

If you cannot get your dreams out into the light, there *are* some things that you can do to lift yourself out of your everyday thinking. Go back to Chapter 1 and look at your beliefs in more detail. Work with your spiritual guides and the prosperity rituals found in the next few chapters. There are also two techniques on pages 79–81 that are very effective.

Prosperity breakout

Step 1

Sit down somewhere quiet with your eyes closed. Imagine that you are floating
out high above your everyday life. You can see yourself in your life down below.

Step 2

Imagine going higher and higher into the air, so that the you below is just a tiny
person from the vantage point of the you looking down. You can see all of your
life – the past, present and future – spread out below you.

Step 3

Imagine that you are a very powerful being. In this position you have the power
to change anything in the timeline below you. Notice how at the moment there
is a direct link between what has happened in the past to what will happen in the
future. The past contains all your different memories and beliefs. You may even
see the past going back farther than this current lifetime into past lives or into
the lives of your parents and grandparents and other ancestors. Notice where on
your timeline there has been an event or incident that has changed the patterns
of thoughts, conscious and unconscious, and therefore what has been attracted
into your life when it comes to prosperity, wealth or money issues.

Step 4

You have a choice to change your destiny. You can change anything on this
timeline. Open up the top of your head (the crown chakra, see page 175).
Imagine that the healing, loving light of the universe is flowing through you
and out through your heart down to the timeline below. Breathe deeply and, as
you exhale and release the breath, imagine that it is full of light energy. See the
energy repair any fractured points on the timeline that need to be sent love and
healing. Imagine that, as you do this, your future is changing as a result. Notice
how your future timeline changes. Perhaps it changes colour or direction, or
even width. From your vantage point, you may observe future events in your
timeline. Let the loving light fill your future, so that your future is free to
become a future of your dreams. You have broken out from your past and no
longer need to be its prisoner. You can make of your future what you will.

Step 5

As you do this, some ideas for your future may spontaneously pop into your mind.
You may also go down and take a closer look at your future. Choose a point in
your timeline that corresponds to a particular date in the future. What dreams
can you see being manifested there? How do you feel about them? If they are
not strong enough yet, imagine that you have the power to turn them to dreams
of pure gold. Shoot a golden light into the event, and change the circumstances
of your future into the best and most prosperous they can possibly be.

Step 6

When you have completed this, gently float back down into your body. Take
a deep breath to ground yourself, and come back into the room by opening
your eyes.

Notice how this exercise frees you up to write down your dreams and gain
clarity about what you really want to manifest in your life.

Lift your vibration

Bringing laughter into your life lifts the vibration of your energy. It shakes off the shackles of your present feelings and frees up your mind to get creative. Watch some comedy. Read a happy book. Dance to some silly music. Do whatever you need to do to get yourself laughing. The more, the better. Once you have spent time having fun, it is time to get creative.

Step 1
Settle down with some coloured pens and paper, and draw a picture of your happy, prosperous future as freely as you would if you were a child.

Step 2
Do this in stages if you like. Use a combination of words and pictures, and stick them all on a big sheet of paper. Draw your own images and add inspiring pictures you have cut from magazines. See what this sparks off in your imagination over the following few days.

Step 3
As your dreams become clearer, start to write them down in more detail.

Live your dreams

Living your dreams is so important to your success in manifesting a prosperous future that I want you to really get into living your dreams *before* they happen. Take a look at everything you have written down in the exercise on the previous pages. Your future is not set. There are so many possibilities for you to create. Is this the future you really want?

Consider each item on your prosperity list (see page 72) in turn. Now imagine that your life contains each of these. How is it going to affect you? What does it feel like? Do you like the person you have become when you have this item?

Project yourself mentally at least ten years in the future. Twenty is good. The farther into the future we can project ourselves, the easier it is to free ourselves from the constraints of the present.

Are you happy? Are you laughing? If not, what can you add to your dream to make it happy and full of lightness and laughter?

There is no need to rush this process. Be sure that you really break the pattern of your particular past, rather than just come up with a list that is full of 'ought tos' or 'shoulds' – or the same generic list as everyone else's on the planet. You do not need to create the dreams of your friends or of your mother or father or anybody else. Free yourself from the past. Let your imagination take you fully into an entirely new way of living, one that goes beyond all your previous limitations. Mentally explore every corner of your dream life. See yourself getting up in the morning. See yourself with your friends. See yourself being happy. See yourself in the career that will help you to create this wealth and prosperous life. See yourself as successful. See what you are buying with your wealth. Imagine that your home is full of beautiful things. See what you are wearing. Imagine what you are doing with your wealth. Notice the activities in which you take part.

The more detail you can find in your dream, the more you can consolidate it in your mind. And the more you live your dreams before they happen, the more successful you will be in manifesting them.

The key to success: feeling

Key to successful manifestation are the pictures you make in your mind's eye of your intentions and also the strength of the feelings you have attached to them. The Law of Attraction works according to thoughts and emotions (see page 23). If you can feel what it will really be like when you have attracted prosperity into your life, you will then get exactly what you have asked for. The more you can feel your future life exactly as if it is really happening to you right now, the more successful you will be at attracting prosperity. This is why it is really important to engage the creative, imaginative part of your mind.

Consider your intentions fully, and really imagine them happening to you as if it is now. Let yourself loose to dream. Use your heart to feel whether something is right or now. Then decide that this will happen and when it will happen. When you do this you create a future energetic memory in the timeline of your life.

The creative part of the universe does not contain a past, present or future. In the spirit universe the time is always now. Imagine your future as if it is happening to you right now and the spirit universe will hear your belief. Then, according to the rules of time and space we live by in this part of the universe, your intention will come to you.

You do not need the how

It is a mistake to think that you need to know every step of how you will make this vision become a reality. As long as you commit to making this vision happen and take some first steps, the universe will help you along with a little bit or a lot of luck.

You can, if you like, break down a vision for you in, say, ten years' time into different intentions/goals that act as stepping stones along the way. One way to do this is to imagine in your mind that you are already in your life in ten years' time. Now look back from that vantage point in the future toward now – the point from where your journey is beginning.

As you look along the path that has taken you from now to the future, notice, if you wish, things that happened along the way that gave you cause for celebration. These things may or may not actually happen. By seeing one possible route or the many possible routes to your dreams, you allow your unconscious trust that you will definitely realize your dreams to grow, and as it grows, your manifestation power is also boosted.

Create your intention list

Your next step to manifesting your vision is to write down your goals/intentions (all of them!). Remember to:

🍂 Give the universe a clear message about how you intend your life to be.

🍂 Take any negatives out of your prosperity lists, for example, don't list what you don't want.

🍂 Focus intently on each area of your life where you have a clear goal by writing an intention statement for each item on your prosperity list as laid out below.

Create intentions for five, ten and twenty years. Some of these intentions will be about what you want to use your wealth for. Some may include a specific amount of money. The key is to remember that money intentions work best not when you are feeling desperate – because then you are vibrating 'lack' thoughts to the universe – but when you are happy and joyful about how you will spend your money.

The rules of intention statements

🍂 Write your intention in the present tense as if it is happening to you **right now** (this way you feel your intention becoming real). **SEE it, FEEL it, HEAR it.** Create a **positive** emotional connection to it.

🍂 Be specific about **WHAT** you want.

🍂 Be clear **WHY** you want this – your intention must be personally compelling for it to have sufficient energetic 'charge' to manifest.

🍂 Be clear **WHEN** you want this. (This helps you to focus clearly on what you will create.)

🍂 Be clear that having this in your life will be **good** – for you and for everyone else who might be impacted by it.

🍂 Decide what you are going to **DO** to make this happen as a **FIRST STEP** (even if the universe may eventually give it to you in another way).

🍂 **WRITE DOWN YOUR INTENTION.** (This ensures that you commit to your intention.)

EXAMPLE

Imagine that one of your intentions is to manifest savings of a specific amount of money within two years. The reason that you want this is for a deposit on a property. You are clear in your mind that having a property will free you up to do other things you want in your life. You see yourself and feel yourself living happily in the property with your family. You imagine that you have beautiful furniture and a joyous life there. You have thought this intention through, including the impact on other parts of your life of paying an ongoing mortgage. The first actions you intend to take toward this are to apply for a new job and to start regular payments into a savings account. You write down a statement like the one on the opposite page.

EXERCISE

YOUR INTENTION STATEMENT

It is 16 March 2020. I have my savings account balance written down in front of me. It shows that I have 'x' amount in my bank account, which has come to me over the period up to this point.

Important: Make sure as you look at this statement that you have a clear picture of it, as if this imagined scene is happening now. Then look at the picture from another angle seeing yourself looking at your bank balance. This should appear as though you are playing back a scene in a movie. Next, decide what part you are going to play in creating this scenario, by writing down at least one first step towards your goal. This should be a step that you intend to make immediately.

My first step is to open a savings account.

SAY THANK YOU

Remember to say thank you in advance to the universe for what it is about to bring into your life. Thanks should always be said because, in one part of the universe, this change has already been created – we just can't see it yet. Every time you create a clear picture and feel it as if it is real, you create a future memory, as real in the universe as a past memory.

Thank you for this already having happened in the best way and to the highest good of all concerned.

THE IDEAL DATE

It definitely helps to put dates to intentions. Putting in place a time frame works to make the intentions more real – with one caveat. It is far better to write down long-term intentions than short-term goals. There is a danger in putting down dates that are too near the present. The focus you keep on your intention is best if it is a 'soft' intention – in other words, so that you remember the date you have set without becoming obsessed or needy of the intention manifesting by that date. Constantly thinking about the date you have set makes you like a cake-watching cook – opening up the oven door every five minutes to check whether your cake is really baking or not. The result with a cake is that it collapses from too much attention. It is the same with your goals. If you keep rechecking them, you create the vibration of doubt, and doubt delays the manifestation of the goal.

SUMMARY

Take the time to decide what you want. What is your vision of a happy, prosperous life? Decide how much money you want. Know why you want this amount. What are you going to use it for?

Next, question yourself. Why is this important? This will clarify your dreams and help you to decide what you are going to devote your efforts toward achieving.

Take what you have brainstormed and turn it into a clear vision and a list of goals/intentions. Make sure that you have worded these positively and have fully imagined what your life will feel like when you have it.

Now let go and trust that these intentions are already a future memory in the creative brain of the universe. They already exist and are just waiting to come into your life. Stay positive, making sure that your beliefs support your intention to receive this future prosperity.

NOTES

CHAPTER 4

Play your part

'A BANK BOOK MAKES GOOD READING –
BETTER THAN SOME NOVELS.'
ENTERTAINER HARRY LAUDER

This is a very practical chapter. Creating your future is teamwork. The universe will help you if you play your part and help to co-create your future. If you just sit there and wait for something to happen, the likelihood is that it will not. If you take the initiative to create the circumstances that you want in your life, you will be rewarded as the universe supports you by bringing you the people and opportunities to take inspired action. As you take action it is important to ensure that your beliefs continue to support what you want to achieve.

Keep developing your loving relationship with the idea of prosperity and business.

In this chapter you will learn:

♣ How to play your part in co-creating your future

♣ How the universe rewards personal responsibility

♣ How to stay receptive to signals from the universe

♣ How to continue developing your loving relationship with wealth.

The gods help those who help themselves

It is true that you do not ever need to know every step of how you are going to achieve your goals, but you do have to keep taking actions and seizing opportunities that come your way. The universe does not help us if we do nothing – only if it sees us taking action toward our goals. It is simply an extension of the premise of giving and receiving. If you expect something to come to meet you, you must make the effort to go to meet it. As the old adage goes, the gods help those who help themselves. People really do help to create their own luck.

The way this works always reminds me of an old joke:

Bob is desperate for money. He prays to God: 'I will do my best to become more religious and practise every day if you can only help me to win the lottery.' He waits by the TV the next day to check his numbers. Not one of his numbers comes up.

Bob is now really desperate. He falls onto his knees and begs, 'God, please help me. If I don't win the lottery tonight, then it is all over. I will go bankrupt and the bailiffs will be at my door. Help me, please.' He watches the lottery numbers again. Nothing. Not even one of his numbers has come up.

A week later Bob prays again, sobbing to God, 'God, you must help me. This is absolutely my last chance. My wife says she will leave me and take the kids. I will lose my house and everything in it. I am begging you, Lord, please help me to win the lottery.'

Suddenly there is a clap of mighty thunder. The clouds part and a deep voice is heard from the heavens.

'Bob. Meet me halfway here. Go and buy a lottery ticket!'

Here's another joke. Not about money this time, but still the same idea – that we must play our part in what happens to us:

A priest was in his church giving a sermon when suddenly it began to rain. It rained and rained, and soon the whole place was flooded. The people started to leave the church because the water was already up to their ankles. The priest kept on preaching while everyone else left. One of the congregation called out to him, 'Sir, you must leave. You will be caught in the floods.'

'Don't worry about me,' answered the priest, smiling happily. 'God will save me.'

Now everyone had left and the water was up to the priest's knees. One of the people of the town drove past in a car and saw the priest standing there through the open door of the church. 'I can help you,' he said to the priest.

'No need, no need,' waved the priest happily. 'God will save me.'

The waters continued to rise. A man in a boat rowed past the church. 'Hey. Swim here and I can help you. You are going to drown,' he called to the priest.

'No, I'm fine,' smiled the priest. 'God will save me.'

The floodwaters rose higher and higher. The priest started to climb onto the roof of the church. At that moment a man in a rescue helicopter flew by and saw the priest there. 'Quick,' he called out. 'Come here before you drown and I will rescue you.'

'I am OK,' the priest said once more. 'Don't bother about me. The Lord will save me.' The pilot tried to persuade him to leave the church, but the priest refused to get onto the helicopter. 'Leave me. God will help me.' Eventually the helicopter flew away.

The waters rose and rose, and sadly the priest was swept into the waters and drowned. The next thing he knew, he was in heaven. The first person he saw was God.

'God, why didn't you save me?' asked the priest. 'Wasn't I a good man? Didn't I pray and pray? Yet you deserted me.'

God replied, 'I sent you a car and a boat and a helicopter. What else did you want me to do?'

Take responsibility for yourself and your future

The wealthy people I have met, those who have held on to their wealth, all have one thing in common. They know that if they lost their wealth, they would make sure that they became wealthy again. How? They did not know at that point. It did not matter really. They simply knew that because they took responsibility for creating wealth the first time around that they could do it again, rather than just rely on luck bringing it to them. This wealth-keeping mindset is shared not only by self-made millionaires and wealthy professionals, but also by many people I know who have inherited wealth. Those lucky individuals divide into two camps: those who just go and spend their inheritance and those who use the money to invest wisely, carrying the wealth forward to the next generation. All of the prosperous individuals I have met around the world have an unshakeable faith that they will create wealth and prosperity by taking action and having a clear vision of their future. They are not swayed by the doubts of those who sit and wait for luck to hit them.

Taking action and taking responsibility are part of a prosperous mindset. This chapter will show you some ways that you can reinforce your abundance and prosperity beliefs through action. This in turn will help the universe to pull your intention into creation.

Take inspired action

You never know exactly how the universe will make your intention manifest, but the good thing is that you do not need to know every single thing that you are going to do to make your intention manifest. The universe will help you.

What is always clear, however, is that the universe rewards action and personal responsibility. Manifesting anything is a joint project between you and the universe. What part will you play in creating the future you want? This is something that a lot of people do not like to dwell on because they hope that, if they do nothing toward realizing their intentions, they will happen anyway. Remember that this is a universe of flow. By giving a service in return for the intention you manifest, the universe brings that intention to you for realization.

You have already outlined in your intention statement (see page 86) some action or service you going to perform. Now it is time to think a little bit more about how you are going to stay on track, focusing on the end goal. Think of every practical action that you take toward your intentions as an investment.

For example, let us take the sample intention in the last chapter (see page 87). It is very clear. You need to get a specific amount of money together within two years for a down payment on a property. How are you going to do this? Well, you know the work you want to do and you have started saving; however, in your mind you cannot see that this is going to be enough.

What do you do next?

You keep your focus on the end prize, and let the universe guide you – by bringing you opportunities to take action, or what I call 'inspired actions'. These opportunities may appear mundane – well, that is because they are. But they have come your way only because of the thoughts and intentions you have put out to the universe. The key is taking personal responsibility for making your intentions happen, which helps you to get creative and notice the opportunities that come your way.

TAKE CARE OF THE MONEY YOU HAVE ALREADY

Here is a good starting point for everyone. Although prosperity is about more than just money, you do need to have a good relationship with your existing money. If this is not the case, take steps to change the situation – it is all part of being grateful for what you have already received.

When you create prosperity there is one big change that is inevitable. You will be much richer than you are now. Many rich people pay others to advise them what to do with their wealth. Others pay accountants and bookkeepers to keep an eye on their current cash flow. That is all very well, but however rich you are, you need to keep an eye on your wealth and guide those who help you. After all, there have been some amazing cases of even the fabulously wealthy overspending and going into debt, even going bankrupt. I could never understand how this happened when I was younger, but it is much clearer to me now, having observed the spending patterns of different people over the years. If you do not stay in charge of the basic details of your finances, it is easy to get carried away with buying things you do not need or to make bad investments – or to let other people take advantage of you.

Do the wealthy throw their money around? Actually, no. Surveys show that the truly wealthy tend to live well within their means. They are not all that fussed about showing off their high status at the expense of wealth. Warren Buffett, one of the most successful investors in the world, is a classic example. He still lives in a relatively modest home despite enormous financial success.

REVERSE PREVIOUS BAD MANAGEMENT

Does neglect pay a part in your financial management? Do you feel trapped by money?

Break any bad financial habits that you have. If you are stuck in a cycle of overdrafts or credit-card debt while earning at least an average salary, it is within your power to make a change. Take a big breath. Sit down and write down what you can do to cut out unnecessary spending. Getting to grips with the details will prevent you from creating more lack thinking (see page 27) and sabotaging the intentions you have set. It breaks the cycle of bad financial decision-making. Write out everyone you owe, such as credit-card or store-card companies, and set an intention/goal with a date by when you will have cleared this debt. Follow the structure of the intention example in the previous chapter (see page 86).

Doing this may involve a life change. Perhaps you will need to rent out a spare room, take on some extra work or give up some luxuries. If it does, realize that the universe will support you.

CASE STUDY: DANNY – TAKING CHARGE OF YOUR FINANCES

A few years ago Danny was in a bad financial situation and felt that things were spiralling out of control. About to go under financially, having lost his job and gone through a divorce, he had to sell his beloved home and move overseas to take the only job he was offered. He really did not want to do it. He knew no one in the country where he was moving to and felt very much alone. What happened? Well, he was forced to make friends quickly, and one of his neighbours introduced him to the woman who was to become his wife, Lizzie, who owned a house far, far nicer than the one he had sold back in the United Kingdom. Danny has been very successful.

Danny now works part-time with his own business, and he and Lizzie live a very contented life. That just would not have happened if it had not been for him taking charge of his finances.

INVEST IN YOUR FUTURE

If you talk to millionaires, one thing many of them have in common is that they invest for the future. They will happily sacrifice rewards in the present for rewards in the future. This is because they believe absolutely in their ability to create their visions.

Even if they do not start with much business or financial know-how, they make sure to acquire it by paying attention. Successful accumulators of wealth research investments. They find out ways to increase their savings income and earn money not just from their salaries, but also as they sleep – from their investments. It helps to remember the following:

- When in doubt, take an action toward your intention. Sitting there doing nothing shows the universe that you are not playing your part. Do not just *try* to do something; stand up and do whatever you think you have the resources to do right now. You will be rewarded for taking responsibility.

- Budget your money and budget your time to keep your life in balance. Plan your income and expenses ahead. Financial independence will be your reward.

- Know what you earn – before and after tax. Know how much money you have available for essentials and how much for luxuries. Is there anything you do not need now that could be better used as savings or for investing toward the future?

- Start up a regular savings account. On a very basic level, hopefully you are going to get paid interest on what is in there. Already you are accumulating wealth.

Love your money

The key to creating wealth and prosperity is to learn to love thinking about what you are going to do with your money.

You need to start to develop a love relationship with investments. You do not have to have a lot of money to begin with; all savings can begin on a shoestring. Begin by developing a good relationship with the idea or energy of money. This ensures that you do not lapse back into lack beliefs (see page 27) because you will feel on top of things. Knowing that you know as much (or more) about money as everybody else helps you to feel that you can be prosperous because it is in your hands.

Having worked in the international financial markets means that I am not afraid of reading about money and business, but many of my friends — and especially my friends who label themselves as 'spiritual' — are very fearful of the idea of money. This is not true in all societies, but nonetheless there are millions of people around the world who are not entirely comfortable with the idea of money. I do understand this. Before I got my first job working with money, I had never picked up a business newspaper in my life. Unlike many of my colleagues, I had not studied economics or business or finance. I certainly could not read a set of accounts, and I had only a very vague idea what a stock was or a bond was. I had to learn on the job very quickly. But I can tell you, it is possible for *anyone* to learn the basics of how money works — and you will feel much better for it. Feel better and you will be in control of your prosperity creation.

KEEP TRACK OF THE MONEY BLESSINGS YOU ALREADY HAVE

Do not just do your accounts once at the end of the financial year. Keep track of how near you are to realizing your goals. This takes commitment, but it also keeps you focused on the end reward. Remember what you focus on is what you get – it is a basic part of the Law of Attraction (see page 23).

If you are someone who sticks everything in a drawer hoping it will go away, stop it! Get all your receipts and money-related papers out, and take a good hard look at them. By keeping track of your finances, you will be able to see when you take a wrong turning and pull yourself back. You will notice if you are spending too much or perhaps earning but not enjoying your life, or perpetuating any other past poor prosperity habits. It is fascinating looking at spending and earning. Do you know how much you spend on coffees during a year or how much interest you earn from your savings? Know where you are now and you will become clearer on where to make changes.

REWARD YOURSELF

Remember your intention is to create financial success in a way that creates more joy in your life. If it helps, give yourself rewards for each small milestone you reach on the way. For example, if your intention is to create, say, £40,000 or $65,000 in two years, and you save £2,000 or $3,250 toward this, tell yourself good things for having done this. Not only will this make you feel good, but the positive feelings will energize your intentions as well, pulling in the positive power of the universe to help you. Our intentions are often many years ahead, so it is important to keep yourself positive and feeling good for the long haul, not just the short sprint. Choose an appropriate way to monitor and reward yourself as you work toward your intentions/goals:

- Perhaps you could create ten percent reward point, or maybe a milestone marking when you are one-third toward your goal.

- Keep a spreadsheet so that you can see how far you have come.

- Write down your 'wins' on a piece of paper and stick it on your wall to remind you of your progress.

- Keep a calendar and, when you have done something toward one of your intentions, draw a big cross through that day. You will be able to see at a quick, satisfying glance just how far you have come in the course of a year.

EXAMINE YOUR WEALTH-CREATING SKILLS

Wealthy people are clever enough to realize that attaining goals is often a team effort. Self-made millionaires, in particular, tend to be independent-minded people. They draw in money by focusing on providing a service they are passionate about and creating an expertise in that area. At the same time they find people to support them in areas in which they are weaker. This is something I would encourage you to do. If in doubt, just ask the universe to bring the right person to you who will help you with X or Y. Keep a look out – the universe will give you an opportunity for action.

At the same time, you can increase your ability to earn. Be really clear with yourself what your skills are. If you are not sure, ask people who know you in a personal and professional context. Do not limit yourself to just asking people in one area of your life because not everybody knows us in the

same way. Our early careers do not always give us the scope to show off all our talents.

If you are lacking skills, get ready to educate yourself – not just about money, but also in any field you love. I was brought up to think of a life in a profession, such as law, or in a traditional business as the only route to future prosperity. This is not the case any longer, especially with the rise of the Web and the interconnectedness of everyone around the globe. There is always a skill that someone somewhere needs and someone somewhere else can fulfil. Examine your hobbies and interests for opportunities to create wealth. After all, who would have thought a short time ago that there would be a company such as eBay, which could be a route to commercial success for many people sitting in their own homes.

LET YOUR PASSION LEAD YOU CLOSER TO PROSPERITY

Be clear about your passions as well as your skills. If you like doing something, you will put way more effort into it but most importantly you will feel good, and as we know, the Law of Attraction works on feelings. By the way, do not worry if finding work you love and can dedicate yourself to one hundred percent to takes a while to explore. Just keep your eye on the end goal of wealth plus joy. Apparently, the average millionaire does not find his or her real flow until reaching their mid-40s. You may or may not intend to be a millionaire, but you can still relax and take your time. If you are not sure what would be perfect for you, keep working hard at whatever you can do to take you nearer to the intentions you have written down (see page 86). If you feel that you are on the right track, you are likely to keep taking action towards what you want. This will reinforce your beliefs that you can attract prosperity, and having these ideas of abundance will keep you attracting the life you want.

FIND A MENTOR

Here is another thing that wealthy people do. They keep learning. They surround themselves with people who can teach them what they need to know. Take a look at someone's friends and you will learn a lot about them. If you cannot find a person in your immediate circle who can teach you, find a virtual mentor. Learn from people you read about or watch on screen.

Spiritual traditions practised around the planet have long passed on wisdom from teacher to student as a natural way of learning over a lifetime. You do not need to be born knowing everything in one go. Life is, as it is always said to be, a journey of discovery. You will gain the knowledge you need to gain as you go along. If you have a focus – your prosperity intention – for what you need to learn, then this can speed things up.

Be receptive

The most important thing you can do to attract money toward you is to be clear about *what* you want. If you are really clear about what your life will be like when you have attracted money, and know why that matters to you, the universe is going to come along with a load of happy surprises in the way you achieve your intention. You can then take action.

Be receptive. Keep an eye out for opportunities. Listen to what people say to you. Seize the networking opportunity or job opening you are offered. Perhaps one day you may get an e-mail out of the blue offering you the chance to train in a new area or to volunteer for the day. Out of this chance comes an encounter with an important businessperson. Twenty years later you have built a business together with a turnover in the millions. Have you ever found that people come back into your life, or into your life for the first time, and open doors for you out of the blue? Some people would call this the power of networking. I think of it also as the universe's way of helping us out when we are moving toward an intention.

These calls from the universe may seem mundane and not 'magic' enough to be 'gifts' as such. The thing is, the universe does not put a big label on an opportunity – 'This is an opportunity you must take' or 'This is the one you created when you wrote your vision down on that bit of paper' – but it does throw us calls to action out of the blue. If we are not receptive to them, they go away. If we are, it speeds up our progress toward our intentions.

Developing a good relationship with money

The actions below are ways for you to reinforce positive beliefs about money and to develop a better relationship with the spirit of money. I used to hate bills coming in. I hated doing my accounts or keeping a close eye on how much money I had in my bank account. I did all these necessary things, but without pleasure and sometimes with a certain amount of fear.

It will really help you to manifest more money if you can develop a good relationship with the spirit, or energy, of money. If you are still unsure or ambivalent about your relationship with money, here are some ways in which you can change the energy of your thoughts about it. They are all very practical, and they will reinforce abundance beliefs (see page 27).

PAY YOUR BILLS WITH JOY

Let's start with bills. How many of us fear that window-faced envelope dropping through the door or the official-looking one with the name of the tax office on the outside? What would it be like if you could free yourself up from worrying about opening your bills and seeing what is inside? I have always made myself rip them open as quickly as possible, even when I did not have much money. It is the sticking plaster principle: get it off quick and it will hurt less. I have many friends who are much more afraid than me, and let their bills fester in their envelopes, unopened in a drawer.

If this is you, why not start making your bill opening and paying into rituals of thanks to the spirit of money. If you feel bad every time you are about to send a cheque off to pay a bill, you are not showing much trust that an abundant flow will come to you. If you pay with joy, you are going to switch on the flow of abundance and attract it toward you.

A bill is a gift of trust. You have already received a service or will receive a service in return for this sum of money. It is a simple energy exchange based on good faith and trust. Paying your bills joyfully is an expression of thanks for the goodwill of the service provider and therefore to the universe, which has enabled this energetic exchange.

Changing your prosperity energy

For a month, get to know the business pages of the newspaper. Make sure that you read them every day; alternatively, read the business news online. If you do not understand the terminology, buy a book or check it out on the Web. Read up about your local economy and the world economy. Do you understand what inflation is? Do you know what is meant by a credit crunch or a recession? If not, do a little studying.

As you do this each day, focus on how you feel. This is a good way to discover any limiting beliefs or negative feelings that you have about money that may be lurking around. Really focus in. After you have read around for a few days, pick one subject.

For example, how about picking the idea of the stock market. Hold the image you have of the stock market in your mind. Really examine it. How do you feel in relation to this concept?

Where are you feeling these feelings? You may notice movement, or warmth or cold, or another sensation in a particular part of your body. Do you perhaps associate particular sounds or even tastes or smells with the term?

How do you feel toward the energy of this idea associated with money? Do any particular thoughts emerge? Take careful note of them.

If any negative thoughts or emotions emerge, dissolve them away. You can do this energetically by imagining that you are opening up the top of your head – the crown chakra (see page 175) – and letting in the highest universal energy, which is the energy of love and light and creative force. Now let that light flow down through your body and out through your heart, dissolving away all the negative beliefs and feelings. See them leave. Feel your emotions turn as you love the idea of, in this example, the stock market. Then say the words 'I love …,' followed by whatever the idea is. It gets easier the more you do it.

Do not worry if this feels a little strange or artificial at first. Learning any new habit takes practice. Love is the highest force in the universe, and by channelling it through you again and again toward any idea with which you have an uneasy or unclear relationship, you can create an entirely new and positive relationship in its stead.

TAKE ACCOUNT OF THE GROUP MIND

As discussed in Chapter 1, group beliefs are very powerful. If you believe something, there is always a certain amount of energy going toward it. If millions of people believe something, obviously a lot more energy goes toward this belief. This can work in your favour. If you want to adopt a new, positive mindset, find a group of people who think in this way and, if you are open, you will find it easy to adopt their beliefs. Soon you will find yourself attracting similar luck, as long as you do not have any other beliefs that are in conflict with this new set of positive or abundant ones.

One example of this was my becoming a member of the international investment community. Despite the fact that I had grown up with very little money, once I was in this new environment, I soon assumed that I could make money because everyone around me did.

Of course such group beliefs can work the other way as well. In other circumstances than those above, I may have thought that I could not charge a particular amount for a service I provided because I would not question the value of what I did in monetary terms when no one else questioned it either. If the group mind has limiting beliefs and you are an open person, you are going to need to take steps to stay away from this negative energy. I found this out as soon as I left my previous profession and for the first time questioned the value of what I did. The exercise on page 110 is a ritual that will help you to get back some power to act outside these limiting beliefs.

Undoing group money and prosperity beliefs

Think about your current profession. What are some of the commonly held money beliefs found in this profession? Are these useful?

Now think about the beliefs about money and prosperity in your country as a whole or associated with your politics or peer group. Are these useful?

Next, think through your life so far. What are the major financial events you have observed? Perhaps you have seen recessions, booms and crashes, including the most recent credit crunch. How have you been affected by these events? Have you managed to stay apart from the group mind? Have you bought into group thinking about your ability to create prosperity in these situations? Has this made you more risk-taking? Less risk-taking?

The truth is that you can make money in any circumstances and create a good life in many circumstances, but it is easy to buy into other people's mindsets and be unable to separate your own thinking from the thinking of others. This is a well-known phenomenon in the financial world. When you are young and just starting out, you are untainted by circumstance. Therefore the investment decisions you take can be quite 'pure' – based on reward, not fear. After you have been through a couple of recessions, on the good side you learn a bit of caution, but on the negative side you may lose your ability to see the opportunities.

Acknowledge your thoughts. Note down any that you think are harming your ability to create prosperity.

Now notice once more how these negative ideas are affecting you on a feeling level. Observe them in your body as emotions with a form to them. Notice any sounds, tastes or smells you associate with them. Take each idea in turn and do this. There is no need to rush; you can do one or two at a time.

If you like, do this in a very meditational way. Sit quietly in a chair or lie down. Close your eyes and really get in touch with the idea – for example, 'recessions harm my ability to earn'. Again, melt away any negative thoughts and feelings using the energy of love in the same way as in the previous exercise (see page 108). With your eyes open or closed, open up your crown chakra and allow the flow of universal energy through to the thoughts and feelings, healing them up with love so that you can let go of them *for ever*, creating a space that you can now fill with fresh new thoughts of your own that support your intention.

You can also write down an abundance belief (see page 27) concerning this subject in advance, and imagine it slotting into the space you have created.

If you have to do this more than once, that is absolutely fine. Practise again and again until you really feel that your emotional reactions have changed and that you can clearly see when and where you have bought into a particular mindset without thinking for yourself first.

SUMMARY

The key message of this chapter is that you are a co-creator of your life. You work together with the universe to bring about your future. Your role is to define what you want and to take responsibility for making your intention or intentions happen by looking out for opportunities to act.

Be clear what service you are offering the universe in return for prosperity. Know your skills and your passions. The universe will then support you by inspiring you to take action – bringing the right events into your life that you can take advantage of as you work toward your intention.

Support this co-creation by continuing to develop your positive relationship with money. Keep track of your finances and kick out bad habits. Next, be receptive – the universe may bring the money to you in unexpected ways.

NOTES

CHAPTER 5

Prosperity rituals

'MEN DO NOT ATTRACT WHAT THEY WANT, BUT
WHAT THEY ARE.'

JAMES ALLEN, *AS A MAN THINKETH*

Life is made up of little rituals that reinforce your ordinary life. We give cards and gifts. We meet up with colleagues or friends. We cook for those we love. We say prayers. Rituals are strong ways of expressing belief in what is important to us.

They make us repeat the same thoughts again and again, reinforcing our conviction that we will attract what we desire. You can make your own rituals or use existing ones from different cultures to boost your new beliefs so that you attract the flow of prosperity into your life.

In this chapter you will learn:

♣ How to make visual prosperity props, which will keep you focused on your intentions

♣ How to create a symbol of your intention, which will draw the energies of it near to you

♣ The power of using real money for rituals.

The rituals help you to change any lingering self-limiting beliefs and boost your trust that you will manifest your intentions, and ultimately the whole vision you have of a prosperous future for yourself. When you repeat the same thought or action again and again, it becomes a habit. Rituals help you to change your inner world – where all your thoughts and emotions are stored – through the power of repetition.

Get clear on your motivation

You can practise any of the rituals within this chapter as they are or, indeed, vary them and make them very personal to you. You can create your own rituals for wealth and prosperity. Whatever rituals you choose to practise, please be very clear about your motivation *before* carrying them out. Be really honest with yourself. You cannot cheat the universe because the universe picks up on every thought you have, conscious or unconscious.

Wealth rituals have been used for millennia. Religious practitioners prayed to their gods for wealth. Magicians used spells and rituals in order to create wealth for themselves, for others or for countries or kingdoms. They did not always work. One of the big reasons is that many magicians were blocked by the belief that it was wrong to use magic to create wealth. If this is a belief you suspect that you might hold, it is really important to examine the reasons for it and change it, otherwise you will not get the results you want from the rituals that follow in this chapter. One of the best ways to change this belief is to get absolutely clear on the reasons you want wealth. Remember, if you know the WHY, you will receive the WHAT (see page 114).

Prosperity props

The first ritual is a very simple one: make yourself a prosperity prop.

Prosperity props are a very easy way for you to keep your focus on your vision. Suppose your goal is to attract a radical change in your way of life, involving a new home within a timeline of five years. That is going to take a large amount of money. Fair enough, you can do it. At the same time, you need to be able to sustain your intention over that five-year period. A prosperity prop is a tangible and visual reminder of your prosperity vision. It should make you feel good when you look at it and be specific enough to bring your particular vision into your mind. The right prosperity prop will help you to maintain your trust that you will attract your vision throughout the five years, even if you cannot see any evidence of it manifesting immediately.

Jim Carrey, the Canadian comic and Hollywood movie star, is said to have had his own prosperity prop before he became famous. The story goes that when he was a young and struggling comedian, he was about to give up on his dream of being a success. He sat down by Los Angeles' Mulholland Drive and wrote himself a cheque for $10 million, and inscribed on it that it was 'for acting services'. He carried the cheque with him as a reminder of what he wanted to achieve. As you know, it worked. By the mid 1990s, Jim Carrey was enormously successful and was able to command fees of millions of dollars per movie.

Making your own prosperity props

Here are some suggestions for prosperity props that are very easy to make and use. You can choose one of the examples listed here or use them as inspiration to tailor a prosperity prop that will most inspire you and help you to keep on track.

WRITE YOURSELF A CHEQUE

Write yourself a cheque for the amount you want to be worth in a few years, time. Postdate it so that it reflects the date by which you want to achieve your intention/goal. For example, write yourself a million-pound or million-dollar cheque for ten years' time. Sign it and address the cheque to yourself.

When you do this, don't just rip a cheque out of your chequebook, fill it in and forget about it. Rituals are powerful because they are acts of concentrated thought and focus. They are about giving you power, and are your expression of devotion and trust in the universe. You must treat them with some reverence.

For instance, you can make a prosperity altar in your home by setting aside a space for all your rituals and place your cheque on it. Regularly energize the space around your altar: light candles, pray over it, make offerings of food and pretty objects, or place photographs there of what you intend to use your money for once you have achieved your goal.

PROSPERITY BOARD

In Chapter 3, it was suggested that you start drawing or cutting out pictures of what you want, to prompt you to draw up a clear vision of your future (see page 81). This is a technique that works for any kind of goal. Even after you have drawn up your vision of your prosperous future, it is still a good idea to keep a prosperity vision board. You can either make a collage or, preferably, use a corkboard or pinboard. Having a prosperity board is a great way to remind yourself on a daily basis that you are already in the process of creating your prosperity goals.

Collages program your unconscious mind. They help you to create focus and direct your thoughts unconsciously toward your goals, triggering the power of the universe to help you manifest those goals. I have been amazed by just how much circumstances that come my way resemble the pictures of places and people on my board.

Get a corkboard or pinboard that you can pin things onto (and some pins!), and start choosing the things you would like to display on your board as your prompts to prosperity. Here are some suggestions:

◆ Start cutting out pictures from magazines that remind you of the life you will be living when you are prosperous. The only rule is that they have to feel personal to you and make you feel good. If in doubt, leave them out.

◆ Get hold of some fake money. There are plenty of board games out there that use quite realistic-looking dollar bills. By the way, it is illegal to photocopy real money in many countries, so stick to the toy stuff. Pick a great wad of paper money, and pin it onto your board. It reminds you that there is always enough money to go around.

◆ Display some Chinese money envelopes – the red paper envelopes you see at Chinese New Year, which are traditionally used for gifts of money (the colour red symbolizes good luck in Chinese culture) – up on your board to remind you to attract wealth.

◆ Chinese symbols of wealth using Chinese characters are also easy to find. Pretty much every Chinese household keeps some sort of symbol up in the home at New Year to remind family members to keep healthy, live long and be prosperous. These symbols make very positive messages to keep on your board.

LOOKING AT YOUR PROSPERITY BOARD

Making a prosperity board is like having a dance of delight with your unconscious every day. Each time you look at it, you will see the person you are going to become one day in the not too distant future. It should reflect the key parts of your prosperous life in the years ahead, showing you what you will be doing, being and having.

Every time you look at it, your unconscious begins to believe that this life is a foregone conclusion, which is why it is so important that the pictures and symbols you pick really make your heart sing when you see them!

The great thing about having the Internet is that you no longer need to rely on accidentally finding a picture in a magazine. You can search on the Internet for pictures by subject or keyword. This means that, if you collect enough images, you can even make a slideshow on your computer of your future. You can set this up so that, when the computer goes into rest mode, it starts flicking through your future life. (By the way, you can also take advantage of your computer's sticky-note program if it has one – if you want to pay particular attention to a goal, put it on a 'sticky note' so that it is right in front of you on your start-up screen when you turn on your computer.)

The good thing about collecting lots of pictures quickly is that it prevents your conscious mind from interfering. And your unconscious mind is more important than your conscious mind here because it is your unconscious mind that runs most of your life. It is your unconscious that will provide the thoughts that the Law of Attraction (see page 23) will use to create your future.

Collect a pile or file folder of images, and move them around until you feel as if they are in the right place. You will know when it does not feel right. Pin the images to your board or stick them on with glue.

If you are not sure about a picture, please just discard it. Why manifest a future that is almost but not quite right? Why not go for what you really want? Think of your prosperity board as a blueprint for your future. Create a balanced life with activities and quiet times and beauty, as well as pictures of all the things on which you are going to spend your new wealth.

As you put together your board and add bits and pieces to it, feel joy and abundance just in the making of it. Make it large and bright and exciting – just like this wonderful prosperous future you are working toward. Remember that the Law of Attraction works on feelings. The more you can believe that your future is possible and probable, the more of it will be attracted to you. By interacting with the universe in this creative way you are saying: 'I know what I want and I am relaxed about how I will achieve it.'

Now decide where you are going to hang your board. If you are in a shared home, try to put it somewhere private where it is mainly you who sees it. It is better if you do not get constant comments from other people on what you have chosen. You can put it near a home altar, or in a bedroom or personal study, or check out the prosperity corner of your home from a feng shui point of view and put it there (see page 124). You can even make a mini-collage and carry it with you in a wallet or purse.

KEY POINTS FOR YOUR PROSPERITY BOARD

♠ Make your future visual: use pictures, not words.

♠ Choose images that are meaningful to you and make you feel good.

♠ Keep it private so that you are not influenced by other people's comments.

♠ Add to your prosperity board whenever you want.

MAKE A PROSPERITY SIGIL

A sigil is an inscribed or painted symbol or image considered to have special power, and is a way of symbolizing your statement of intent. The Law of Attraction responds to the pictures you make in your brain. A sigil is a very powerful symbol of a personal intention that means something only to the person who has made it.

Here's how it works. Suppose that you intend to attract 15,000 for a new car. You write out an intention such as the following:

It is my intention to have fifteen thousand with which I will buy a new car by 30 June.

Notice that although this is a short-term intention (within a year), it is still specific and measurable, and so is something you can focus on with ease. It is also realistic because you have thought about the cost of a new car and why you want it, and your intention has a clear, precise timing associated with it. It is as a result a very believable – possible and plausible – goal.

To make your sigil, you now list all the letters in the statement of intent, then delete any repeated letters.

The statement above reduces to:

Itsmyneohavfudwcbr30j

Now you take hold of all your creativity and make a drawing or symbolic interpretation out of this combination of letters. The symbol should be simplified so that you can see the elements within it and it is also easy to remember.

I sometimes like to make my sigils look like a little cartoon picture of a made-up animal or person. If you anthropomorphize your symbols, you will find that they are very easy to remember. It is entirely up to you and your creativity and imagination.

Next put your energy into the sigil. Sit with the piece of paper in your hands and think about what it symbolizes. See your intention being realized and block out any other thoughts as you do this. You are pouring energy into your intention.

WHERE TO PUT YOUR SIGIL

You can now pin the sigil to your prosperity board, or you can burn the paper
the sigil is on and thus release attachment to the intention, which symbolizes
your trust that your intention will be realised through the Law of Attraction.

USING YOUR SIGIL AS A MANTRA

Assuming that you have not burned your sigil, you can also use your sigil as a
mantra. Chanting a word that has meaning again and again acts as an attraction
to the vibration of the intention it symbolizes.

USING YOUR SIGIL FOR BUSINESS

A sigil is such a powerful symbol that you can use it in your business as well.
Suppose that you have an intention to create a certain amount of money out
of your next sales campaign. In that case, follow the instructions above. Make
sure that you have a clear outcome for your campaign. Distil this down into an
intention. See the intention in your mind as if it has already happened. Make
sure that all your beliefs are lined up to enable this result. If you have any doubts,
as always, change the intention or change your beliefs by following the process in
Chapter 1.

Next, take the letters of the intention and make a new sigil. Put this sigil on
any sales literature going out to your clients. As the literature is dispatched, keep
the sigil in your mind's eye as a way of reminding yourself to focus on your
intention being manifested. Take action. Ring your clients. Follow up in the
usual way. Notice the results.

Feng shui and prosperity

Feng shui is the ancient Chinese art of placement. It teaches how the arrangement of an environment or home can affect the flow of *qi* (*ch'i*), or universal energy, either negatively or positively. By changing the arrangement of objects within your home, you can attract more luck, happiness, love or wealth.

WATER

Walk into many Chinese offices and businesses, and you will see a fish tank by the entrance. A fish tank, water plant or water feature or fountain just inside the entrance to your home or bedroom door is seen as a sure-fire way of attracting wealth. Water flowing into a pool symbolizes the flow of wealth accumulating in your life. If you employ a feng shui consultant, he or she will be able to tell you other places in your home where you can put glasses of water to attract wealth. In some systems this varies from year to year and is worked out on the basis of a grid system.

BELLS

The sound of bells ringing tells you that good news is on its way. You can buy small metal bells, which you can tie together with red thread or ribbon. Hang these on the door to your home or office, either inside or out, and each time the door is opened it brings in good luck and prosperity.

CHINESE COINS

Nowadays it is relatively easy to get hold of I Ching coins outside China for feng shui purposes. These are the old-style Chinese coins with a hole in the middle of them. Tie three coins together with a suitable length of red ribbon eight inches long (eight traditionally being considered an auspicious number by the Chinese), and hang the coins inside your front door or put them inside your handbag or perhaps a briefcase you carry with you for business. This traditionally brings you a never-ending flow of income. The reason is that, in Chinese culture, the number three symbolizes the coming together of the energies of heaven, earth and man – in other words, you draw on the creativity of heaven to bring you wealth on earth.

CLUTTER CLEARING

In Chinese thinking *qi* – the universal source of energy and giver of life – needs to flow. Clutter in the home blocks the *qi* flow. Where *qi* is blocked it stops the flow of luck into your life. Once you start clearing away the clutter in your home, you will find that you also unclutter your mind.

We often hold on to things we do not really like any more because we think that we will not be able to afford something new and better. Well, the very act of holding on to the old thing you do not like will ensure that you do not get something better in its place. Think of it like this. You are carrying around in your mind the image of all the things in your home – things you like, things you love, things you do not like. If you think about something you own, you can conjure up its image immediately. It is filed away in your amazing brain. What do you feel when you think about the things in your home? How many are there because you love them and how many are there just because they always have been there? The old saying is true. A cluttered home really does make a cluttered mind. Why not throw out all the things you do not really love and see how free you feel? It is tremendously liberating. As you think of each item you want to get rid of, think about who you can give it to who will love receiving it. Give your old things away to a charity, for example, and by liberating these items from your home you free their energy to bring blessings to another home.

The power of using real money

Money is simply a symbol. That wad of cash you have in your wallet or those coins you have in your purse are symbols. Whether it be a dollar, a pound sterling, a euro, a rupee, a yuan or a yen, it is a promise to transfer to the holder a particular amount of value in return for the slip of paper or circle of metal. Currencies are based on trust. That mix of base metals in the coin is not worth what it says on the outside, nor is that piece of paper in itself worth any more than any other piece of paper, except for the fact that we trust the bank that has issued it to honour its promise to give us certain value in return. The power of this trust makes millions of people throughout the world work hard to get more of these pieces of paper and coins. Each note and coin holds enormous power as a result of all the human energy that goes into it. This makes real money very powerful as a tool for prosperity rituals. True, it is in reality as much a symbol as writing yourself a cheque or using fake game money, but the power of millions of minds forming an energetic connection with this symbol cannot be underestimated.

Take a note from your purse or wallet, and look at it. What do you feel as you handle it? What are your associations with it? How willingly would you just give that note away? How much would you like more of these notes or coins? Using this strong mental and emotional connection we have with cold, hard cash is a great way to learn about our money beliefs and a way to attract prosperity.

PROSPERITY TALISMANS

One way to harness the energetic power attached to money is to make yourself a talisman. A talisman is an object or piece of jewellery that works as a good-luck charm. A talisman works because of the energy and intent you put into it. Talismans have been used for many thousands of years for everything from attracting love to warding off evil spirits. Making a talisman using real money provides you with all the emotional and mental associations you need every day to remind your unconscious to focus on creating your intention. Below are two different ways of making talismans: the first is a talisman you can keep on display in your home or office, while the second is a pendant for wearing around your neck.

ARTWORK TALISMAN

Take one or two different paper notes. If you like, you can write your prosperity sigil (see page 122) on the back of each note.

Make a shape out of your note so that it is transformed into a beautiful object that you can look at every day. At home I have two hangings that are made in this way. They look like art, but they are actually made of money and work on the brain as money symbols. If you are not a natural artist, track down an origami book or look up on the Web how to create origami – the Japanese art of paper folding. There are many different shapes you can make with origami, from basic flowers and cranes to more elaborate creations.

If you find you have a particular talent for origami, why not choose to make an animal that represents wealth for you, or perhaps a symbol of what you are going to buy with your wealth? Fold your bill or bills into the appropriate shape. Put your completed talisman somewhere you can see it every day – perhaps the desk from which you work or an area of your home or work space that is a key part of your day.

PROSPERITY PENDANTS

Why not use a real paper note to make a talisman that you can wear? Again, you can mix rituals and write your sigil (see page 122) on the back of this note if you wish. This will make it even more powerful. There are various ways in which you can do this:

- Take an empty locket and put a real banknote inside it with your prosperity intention or sigil written on the back of the note.

- Take a crystal (see the box on page 130 for crystals particularly associated with prosperity). Wrap the crystal in the paper note and use picture wire or ribbon to bind the money to the crystal.

- Take two pieces of card or similar craft material. Cut them to your desired shape and decorate them in whatever colours and designs you feel drawn to as symbolizing wealth and abundance. Now put the note between the two layers of card and glue them or fix them together. Put a hole in the finished shape and hang it from a necklace or key ring to make a talisman that you can see every day.

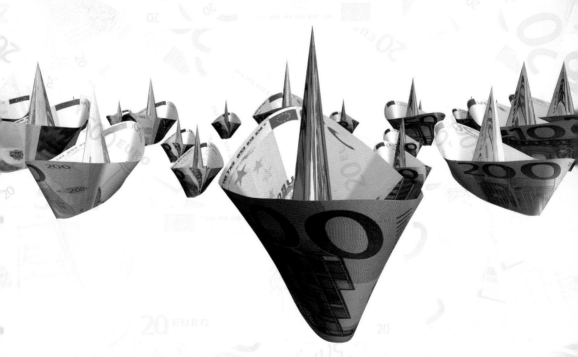

CRYSTALS TRADITIONALLY ASSOCIATED WITH PROSPERITY

Amethyst
Brings you business success, while at the same time opening you up spiritually, so that you are willing to share your success and abundance with others.

Tiger's-eye or tigereye
Attracts people to you who will help you to build your prosperity, as well as your career, and attracts luck generally.

Carnelian
Helps you to actualize your dreams by taking action.

Citrine
Helps you to acquire and keep wealth.

Jade
Is the stone most associated with wealth in Chinese culture. It is considered very auspicious.

Peridot
Brings money and opportunity.

Red garnet
Is particularly good for bringing abundance to women.

Fluorite
Helps you to use your creativity as a way of creating more wealth and prosperity.

Ruby
Helps you to gain wealth and also protects against its loss.

Topaz
Gets rid of doubts and opens the door of opportunity for you.

Bloodstone
Helps to banish poverty consciousness, so that all kinds of abundance can flow into your life.

Quartz crystals
Are amplifiers of other crystals, prayers and visualizations.

PROSPERITY BOTTLE

Putting symbols of what you want to attract in a bottle is a very old idea. Find a pretty bottle with a cork. A coloured bottle works well. You could choose a gold or silver one, for example, because of the obvious association with the valuable metals. Purple is also associated with prosperity, so you could paint your bottle in this colour if it appeals. It is important to use a cork that can be taken out as needed, so that you can add things to your bottle.

Wash the bottle and, in your mind's eye, see white light coming down from the highest source in the universe to clean all old energies out of your bottle. Your bottle can contain any sort of charm, scent, herb or crystal that has associations with prosperity. In addition to your choice of charm, add your real money (coins work best in this case), as well as your sigil (see page 122) or statement of your prosperity intentions (see page 86).

Choose an essential oil and plant traditionally associated with prosperity (some examples are given in the box on page 132). Add them to your bottle and, when it is ready, cork it up. Light a gold candle to say thank you to the energy of the universe in bringing you prosperity with this symbol you have created.

You can put your prosperity bottle on an altar or by the entrance to your home where you will see it every day. Keep adding coins to your bottle at regular intervals. As you do this, thank the powers in the universe for bringing you prosperity and ask that all the money you give to the bottle comes back multiplied in the form of a flow of wealth into your life. When you do this, it is important to keep the intention that you will play your part in the bargain by putting in the effort into creating the life that you want to live. In return the universe will put in the energy to help you.

ESSENTIAL OILS AND PLANTS TRADITIONALLY ASSOCIATED WITH PROSPERITY

Essential oils

- Eucalyptus
- Clary sage
- Yarrow
- Patchouli

Plants

- Geranium
- Chamomile
- Basil
- Garlic

Prosperity piggy bank

Your prosperity piggy bank does not have to be shaped like a pig, even though pigs do have positive associations with wealth in some cultures. All you have to do is to choose some kind of jar, bowl or even bag in which to store money. The difference with this ritual and the one with the prosperity bottle is that you get to use the money you put inside.

Create a sacred space to carry out the ritual. Find a spot in your home or in your garden where you can light candles and create a place to focus on the ritual. Call in any angels or prosperity deities (see page 136) to help you with the ritual. You can do this by yourself or as a group with friends. Working with a group can help to raise the energy of an intention. To raise the energetic vibration of the space, meditate, play some beautiful music or dance to bring in joyful emotions. As you begin the ritual, this positivity will infect every aspect of it.

Take a banknote out of your purse or wallet. It can be a dollar, pound or any currency you regularly use in real life. Hold it in your hands in this sacred space, and truly appreciate it. It is a means for you to get what you want in your life. Feel it, smell it, notice all the patterns and pictures on the bill.

Now think about what you would like to manifest in your life once you have more of these notes. Be really clear and state your intention out loud. This paper note will become a symbol of your intention. Ask the spiritual helpers present to help you to manifest this intention. If you like, you can add a sigil (see page 122) to the note as well. Place the note in your chosen receptacle. I like to add a separate note for each intention I have – this means that I have put exactly the same energy into each of the intentions, and it reminds me to focus on everything, not just one intention to the exclusion of others.

After you have put the money in the container, ask the universe to begin to multiply the money, so that you are showered with abundance in your life and every intention you have will be realized. Thank the universe in advance for these intentions being realized at some point in the future. Use only the money from the prosperity piggy bank to take steps toward your intentions. For example, if your aim is to save the money to buy a house, use one of the notes to open a bank account. Your intention is that the bank account will be filled with money as this particular note is showered with more and more similar notes. Use the money from your piggy bank only for things that are directly connected with your prosperity path.

SUMMARY

There are many rituals you can use to boost your prosperity intentions. Choose the ones to which you feel most attuned – those that feel right for you. These are very personal habits. Vary the rituals you use, or stick to the one with which you feel the most comfortable.

Why not make a prosperity board, so that you have a visual and emotional link to your goals? Make a prosperity altar and write yourself a cheque for a million pounds or dollars – a promise of your future earnings.

Make sigils to keep around the home or use to boost your business.

Use real money and crystals to create prosperity props – a prosperity bottle, talisman or pendant – or start saving and spending from your prosperity piggy bank.

NOTES

CHAPTER 6

Your prosperity helpers

'A WISE MAN SHOULD HAVE MONEY IN HIS HEAD,
BUT NOT IN HIS HEART.'

JONATHAN SWIFT

The invisible spiritual world has many helpers available to us, whatever our day-to-day needs and concerns. You may already be familiar with the idea of guides or angels to whom you can turn for help in times of need. You do not need to be initiated into a particular religion to call on their help. You need only to connect with them by desiring them to come into your life, then ask them for help. The energy of many people maintains the connection between these highest energies and our world. The connection is particularly strong because the thoughts about these deities and helpers are so positive.

In this chapter you will learn about:

♣ The two Hindu deities who can help you to create abundance in your life and undo blocks and obstacles

♣ The Chinese god of prosperity

♣ The Celtic bringer of life and her faery children, who can help you to create a wonderful life

♣ A meditation to meet your personal prosperity guide.

When millions of people point their thoughts into one idea – in this case a higher being or deity – the power of this spiritual helper grows.

How to choose your prosperity helper

Deities from more than one tradition or religion are described here. You do not have to be religious as such to benefit from building a relationship with them. These are all spiritual helpers who, it is believed, are available to you, no matter what your background is. If you have never before worked with higher energies or guides in any form, take your time to read about these helpers. See what your gut reaction is to working with them. It is important that, whatever you do to help you manifest your goals, you do it with your heart fully engaged. If you are not comfortable with any particular ritual, there is absolutely no point practising it because your inner conflict will produce muddled results.

Be careful not to let either your head or greed override your heart or emotions. Remember that the Law of Attraction does work on thoughts, but always in conjunction with feelings. If you do one thing while you feel another, your feelings will produce the end result.

If you are drawn to a particular deity or guide, talk to them regularly, read up about them, keep pictures of them, celebrate their festival days and think of them as a spiritual parent, or protector or friend. They are always willing to open up a relationship with you.

WHAT CAN YOU EXPECT TO HAPPEN?

These helpers are spiritual beings, which means that they can communicate with you and help you in more than one way. They may alert you to any blocks that are preventing you from manifesting prosperity. They may open up opportunities for you to take action and in so doing manifest your goals.

HOW DO THEY COMMUNICATE?

These energetic beings have the power to put people or circumstances on our path that can help us. They may also communicate at night through dreams or during the day by showing us an image or giving us a word message within a meditation. If you use Tarot cards or any kind of divination tool, the helpers will bring you the messages you need through these.

You may also receive clues in your environment. For example, imagine you are trying to make up your mind about whether to take a job that may or may not bring you wealth. You ask your chosen spiritual helper for advice. As you venture out into town to buy your groceries, you see a billboard right in front of you. It says, 'Go for it!' in large letters. Is this a message for you? You are not sure. You pass a store selling sporting goods. You see the same message on a poster. The slogan may be for a well-known manufacturer, but you are noticing it strongly because the universe is communicating with you.

The goddess Lakshmi

The goddess Lakshmi is the household goddess of most Hindu families, and so is worshipped by millions of people around the globe. The word 'Lakshmi' comes from a Sanskrit word meaning 'goal', and she is the goddess of wealth and prosperity – not only material wealth and prosperity, but also spiritual. She is worshipped daily and also has the month of October dedicated to her. If you think about it, this means that each day millions of people are pouring their energy and belief into her, making her a very powerful helper for you.

Lakshmi is one of the oldest goddesses. She was certainly worshipped as long as six thousand years ago, although originally she may have been an earth mother deity, before being brought into the Hindu group of gods and goddesses. In mythology, she is the wife of Lord Vishnu, the Hindu sun god. It was said that she came out of the churning ocean bringing gifts and was so beautiful that all the gods wanted her.

In pictures, you will see Lakshmi depicted as a beautiful woman with four arms and four hands. She stands or sits on a lotus, and also holds a lotus bud – the symbol of beauty and purity. Gold coins flow from her hands. She wears gold and red clothing. Gold is an indicator of prosperity and red is a symbol of activity. In mythology the wealth Lakshmi brings supports creation. It is an interesting image because it promises a flow of abundant wealth and, at the same time, the lotus Lakshmi stands on symbolizes the idea that there is more than just material wealth to aim for in the world. In other words, it is good to create wealth, but not at the expense of other parts of life. She can also help you to find a meaningful career and fulfilment as a means to creating wealth.

Sometimes there are two elephants standing next to the goddess Lakshmi. Elephants represent the idea of gaining fame or a name because of wealth. They are present in the image to remind us that you should not go after wealth simply to gain a name or fame for yourself, but so that you can share it around and do good things in the world. In other words, prosperity should bring joy to you and all around you.

The good thing about Lakshmi is that she is available as a spiritual energy helper to everyone, regardless of your belief system. If you ask her for help, she will bring you help, especially if you are in dire financial need.

ASKING LAKSHMI FOR HELP

First of all, you need to create your personal connection and relationship with Lakshmi. Start reading about her, her mythology, her character and the help she can give. There are many sources online and in books because she is such a popular goddess, and even in the most orthodox thinking she is open to helping all of us.

YOUR PERSONAL PROSPERITY SHRINE

If you want to create a devotional relationship with Lakshmi, you can create a little shrine to her. Put her image on your altar, if you like. Make sure that you clean the image by bringing light down from the universe (see page 108), and imagine it taking away any energy that does not belong to the image.

When you ask for energy from the universe in one form, it is good to give it back in another. You can make an offering to Lakshmi in return for the help she gives you. She likes offerings of sandalwood incense, fruit, flowers, money, milk, shells, candles, yogurt, sweets and candies, or sweet things.

If you offer Lakshmi money, it can either be real currency that you put on your altar or fake paper money to symbolize the real thing. She is also associated with the colours red, gold, white and green, so you can also give her offerings in any of these colours.

Place her offerings around her image on the altar.

THE SHRI YANTRA

It is also a good idea to get hold of a picture of the Shri Yantra. You do not necessarily have to go out to buy a copy of this nowadays because there are plenty of images available on the Web.

The Shri Yantra is a symbol of the goddess Lakshmi and also the union of divine feminine and divine masculine, or non-duality. It is a powerful symbol of devotion that teaches concentration of the mind. It is not specifically used for wealth manifesting, but regular meditation with the Shri Yantra can help you focus and gain inner power. It is composed of nine interlocking triangles, which in turn form 43 smaller triangles. The Yantra shows the point between the universe of matter and the universe of spirit or creation, the route through which everything moves from an idea to manifest in reality. You can bring the goddess energy into the Yantra through your offerings and mantras.

NOTES TO SELF

- By feeling gratitude before you receive, you show your faith that the prosperity you seek will cross that dividing point shown on the Shri Yantra. It moves from being an idea in the unmanifest universe to a reality in this world of matter. Ask that whatever is given to you be to your highest good and also to the good and happiness of all. Health, wealth, joy to all.

- Prosperity is a flow. As you receive the blessings of wealth from Lakshmi, give to others. Lakshmi does not like greedy people. She likes you to give to others and share your good fortune.

- Both remain respectful of the goddess and have fun with her. Your relationship with her is a devotional one; at the same time, the spirit world likes light energies such as joy and laughter. Honour Lakshmi by making regular offerings to her shrine and also through devotions during the times of her special festivals, including the full moon.

Active ritual to bring in the goddess

Using a mantra to call or 'invoke' Lakshmi draws her energy near to you. There are many different ones. I like the mantra below:

Om Shring Hring Kling Tribhuvan Mahalakshmyai Asmaakam Daaridray Naashay Prachur Dhan Dehi Dehi Kling Hring Shring Om

Traditionally this mantra is chanted 108 times to bring in the energy most powerfully. If you have never chanted in another language before, this is something you may wish to practise gradually.

As you ask the goddess to come near, you may feel the energy around you change. As soon as you feel her presence, ask for her help. Remember that she will always want to help you because that is her energy and purpose. You can also use sound to bring up the energies. I have a pair of Tibetan bells that I ring to raise energy. You could also use recordings of chants to Lakshmi, which you can play as you think about bringing Lakshmi into your shrine.

When you feel the shift in energies, spend some time meditating with her. Sit quietly and communicate with her about what you want and why. Explain to her what benefits to your life her blessings of material wealth will bring to you.

You can call on Lakshmi at any time. As you call on her, imagine that your wishes have already been granted by her divine power.

Feel gratitude toward Lakshmi with the prayer of thanks, *Om Nameh Lakshmi Nameh* or the prayer of peace *Om Shanti Shiva Shakti*, for granting these wishes.

The god Ganesh

Although Lakshmi is the main goddess I ask for help on prosperity matters, I also make appeals to the Hindu god Ganesh, who helps to remove obstacles around abundance. Ganesh is the elephant-headed deity and the god of wisdom, abundance and prosperity. In mythology he is the child of Shiva, the supreme being. He was born with an ample body that is said to hold within it all the matter of the universe. Vishnu, the Hindu god of love, gave Ganesh his elephant head. He is a happy, loving, sweet and protective god. His birthday is celebrated sometime in August or September, according to the lunar calendar.

You can ask Ganesh for help with any fear or obstacle you encounter. He is also the god able to grant success. His energy is linked to the movement of energy up and down the chakras (see page 175) and the intellectual mind. This energy makes him very able to help us with everyday concerns.

In some depictions of Ganesh, he holds a bowl of sweet treats in one hand and a noose and goad (a long stick with a pointed end) in another. He uses the goad to push obstacles away from you. He has four arms, which symbolize the vast power he has at his disposal to help you. If you set off down the wrong path, Ganesh will put up obstacles to stop you from proceeding.

ASKING GANESH FOR HELP

Form your relationship with Ganesh by reading everything you can about him and getting hold of an image or picture of Ganesh that you can keep on your altar. He likes to receive sweet things as offerings, especially chocolate. You can also give him flowers and incense.

To bring in the energy of Ganesh, stand in front of your altar if you are in your home. Otherwise bring his image into your mind. Call his name. Now talk to him. He will not answer in words, but he will start to bring events and people into your life to help you with whatever obstacles you are encountering. Tell him your worries and the questions you have, and he will brush aside the obstacles with his goad and open up new opportunities for abundance.

The name Ganesh is very powerful. The most frequently used prosperity mantra linked to Ganesh is below. Say it every day, and see what changes come into your life in relation to money and prosperity.

Om Shri Ganeshaya Namah

Mantras are not ordinary words. Their sounds link you energetically to the higher vibrations of the spiritual universe. If you are experiencing real blocks when it comes to money, chant the mantra above more than once a day – in the morning and at night. At the same time, visualize money and your prosperity intentions manifesting in your life on this earth plane.

Lu Xing – the Chinese god of prosperity

There are three gods generally found together in Chinese images and statues: Fu Xing, the god of happiness, Lu Xing, the god of prosperity, and Shou Xing, the god of longevity. *Xing* is the Chinese word for 'star' and is sometimes written as *Hsing*. If you have happiness, prosperity and longevity, you will have a very good life in Chinese thinking, so these gods work together and are often referred to simply as Fu Lu Shou. You will find them in folk temples in China and throughout Southeast Asia. They will sometimes be represented by statues, and sometimes the Chinese characters for the three gods will appear on banners near the main temple altar. Lu Xing is sometimes shown riding a stag – an animal that can leap up and over mountainous obstacles. He is also drawn holding a sceptre of power.

Lu Xing is particularly helpful to you if you want a promotion or a salary rise. If you are seeking to earn more wealth through your business or by advancing your career, ask Lu Xing for help when you are looking for work as well. He will bring you prosperity, but only if you work hard and help yourself first. His energy is linked to being industrious.

ASKING LU XING FOR HELP

Nowadays it is very easy to get hold of little statues of the three gods Fu Lu Shou from Chinese specialty stores outside Asia. Place the three gods on your altar or have an image of the Chinese characters on your prosperity board (see page 119). In Chinese businesses and homes, these statues are often placed, according to feng shui guidelines, by the entrance to the home or office to attract good luck into the building and the owner's life. Do not separate the gods from one another, but instead give thanks to all three for the benefits they bring into your life. If you have a particular issue you want Lu Xing to help you with, hold his image in your mind and ask him to bring you help.

Danu – the Celtic creator goddess

Danu (also known as Don, Anu or Dana) is the Celtic creator goddess. The river Danube is named after her. Danu is the mother goddess and as such is a goddess of fertility and abundance, as well as protection. She was also known as Brigantia in the Celtic religion of Late Antiquity, and her legend has evolved in Irish legend to link with that of Saint Bride, or Saint Brighid, in Christianity.

Danu's original worshippers were the Tuatha Dé Danann, the children of Danu, whom it is said retreated to the hills of Ireland, where they became the immortal 'faerie folk'. She is therefore considered the protector of faeries. It is said that the Tuatha Dé Danann were originally alchemists – those who were able to change base metals to gold.

Danu has a very strong feminine energy, so you may be particularly drawn to her if you are a woman; however, there is a balance in all energies and therefore Danu also contains masculine power. As the mother goddess, she is immensely powerful.

ASKING DANU AND THE TUATHA DÉ DANANN FOR HELP

As well as for helping create abundance in your life, Danu can be called upon for help on matters of fertility and self-esteem. If you have issues about deserving prosperity, then she is the right goddess for you to tune into to help you to overcome any blocking or lack beliefs (see pages 27–28).

Danu is associated with the faery kingdom, especially Irish faeries or leprechauns, so you can call on their help through her. Some traditions say that there are elementals, or faeries, all around us.

While many of us are used to asking deities or angels for help, belief in faeries is less widespread nowadays. In magical traditions, faeries are said to exist in the invisible planes and so cannot be seen unless you have second sight. Some sensitive people may not see faeries, but they can nevertheless sense their presence because faeries will move objects around the home.

If this view of the spirit world resonates with you, develop a relationship with not only Danu, but also the faeries, and ask them to help you to find prosperity. Leprechauns in mythology have great wealth, which they hide away at the end of the rainbow. Ask Danu to bring you wealth as she brought it to her faery children. Imagine an abundance of wealth flowing toward you. Feel what it feels like as this wealth enhances your life in every way.

If you would like to work with the faeries, you must remember they are said to be as mischievous as depicted in fairy tales. They are also wary of human beings. As children of Mother Earth, they need to know that you care about the earth if you are to make friends with them. Keep plants in your home, cultivate and tend your garden and be kind to the animals and birds around your home.

Find a quiet spot to meditate in your garden. You can even dedicate a spot to the faeries. If you do not have a garden, find a quiet place of nature. As you relax, tell the faeries that you would like to communicate with them, and see what thoughts come into your mind. Start to forge a connection with them, but always remain aware that they have a dark side and can play tricks on unsuspecting humans. Connection with the faeries is not as elevated an energetic connection as you will have with a deity.

I suggest that you also get hold of some faery cards and ask to link into their energy. You can ask the cards to bring you answers relating to any questions you have concerning your prosperity intentions or any blocks or inner issues that have manifested. Just hold the cards in your hand and ask the question. Imagine that Danu is with you as protector of the faeries, so that they know that they must help you. Now pick a card from the pack. The principle is just the same as using a Tarot deck.

Remember that every inner issue preventing you from having immediate wealth can be transmuted into something positive – just as the alchemists are said to have transmuted base metals into gold. The faeries will show you how.

Faery cards can get a little frisky – just like the faeries themselves. I have found that when I handle a deck a card often jumps out of the pack. If this happens to you, pick another card as well but pay particular attention to the card that has jumped out at you. It is always fascinating to see what answer it brings. You can interpret the picture yourself or use the pack's guide.

Making your own faery card pack

If you cannot find any faery cards that you like, you can make your own. This is done by a process of tuning into your intuition and working totally creatively.

Step 1
Get hold of some index cards or plain cards, and some coloured pens.

Step 2
Close your eyes and take a few big, deep breaths to relax yourself. Next, imagine yourself in a quiet place in nature. If you have already designated a part of your garden as a faery meeting place, choose to be there in your mind's eye.

Step 3
Now, still with your eyes closed, imagine the light of the universe coming in and opening up your third eye. This is the point between your eyebrows through which you can have second sight or the ability to see beyond the normal five senses.

Step 4
In your mind, and keeping your eyes closed, I look around this place of nature. Ask that any faeries present give you a glimpse of their shape and form, in a way that is easy and pleasant for you to view them. You may or may not see them at this point.

Step 5
Now open your eyes. Taking a pen in your hand, begin to draw a picture of a faery on a piece of card. Whether it is coming directly from your meditation or even if you think it is just coming out of your imagination, let the drawing flow onto the paper.

You can draw one or more pictures at a session. Draw until the creative urge runs out. To finish each session, in your mind's eye, close up your third eye. Imagine it like an open lotus. To open it, you open up the petals, so that you can see the whole flower. To close it, you fold the petals back in, so that they form a tight, furled bud.

If you repeat this process over days, weeks or months, you will end up with your own 'inspired' pack of faery cards. Each time you use them, they will give you a very personal message because your emotions and vibration will be so linked with them.

Ask the pack a question and pick a card. To interpret the message, let images and words float down into your mind. An idea will spontaneously come to you. If the message is not clear, place the card by your bedside. Ask the faeries to help you to dream the answer to your question. When you awake, take note of the thoughts that have come into your mind.

Meditation to meet your personal spiritual guide

As well as gods and goddesses, a personal guide will also be present in the spiritual world who can help you with any issues you have concerning prosperity. This may or may not be the same guide who is there to help you with other areas of your life.

Get to know your guide as you begin your prosperity manifestation because this will help you to maintain a strong link with the spirit world, as well as helping you with any changes you need to make in your attitude towards prosperity.

Step 1
Sit or lie down in a quiet place where you will not be disturbed.

Step 2
Close your eyes and make sure that you are comfortable. In your mind's eye, open up each of your chakras from the bottom up (see page 175). See the petals of each chakra opening up to show the beauty of the flower and receive the energy of the universe.

Step 3
Now take three deep breaths in through your nose and out through your mouth. As you exhale feel the breath relax every muscle of your body.

Step 4
Feel your legs and arms relax, then your fingers and toes, then in turn your neck and head. You are now ready to be guided into meeting your personal spiritual guide.

Step 5
See in front of you a path. All around you there is natural beauty and greenery. As you walk down this path, let your senses take in the beauty of this green and pleasant place. Notice the grass and the flowers and the trees. Notice the birds singing in the distance. Notice whether there are any tiny clouds in the sky. Feel the ground under your feet. Feel the sun shining on you as you walk. The sun lights the path ahead of you.

Step 6

Soon you come to a beautiful little bubbling brook. You see a little wooden bridge. Walk over it, and you will find that the path takes you to a pyramid. The sides of the pyramid are made of clear crystal.

Step 7

Enter the pyramid and sit down. There are two seats next to each other. Sit in one of them, and ask your guide to join you in the other seat. You may feel or see your guide entering. Your guide may come in a human-looking form. You may see the whole of the guide or just have a flash of his or her feet or face, or some other part of his or her body. If you are not experiencing any contact, gently look up at the point between your eyebrows (your third eye) to activate your second sight.

Step 8

Introduce yourself to your guide, and see whether he or she introduces himself or herself to you.

Step 9

As you sit quietly next to your guide, this is your opportunity to ask your guide any questions you have about blocks or intentions. You can ask the best way to make changes in your life or ask questions relating to life purpose or any of your manifestation intentions.

Step 10

When your guide answers you, he or she may do so by letting ideas or images come into your mind or he or she may give you a gift. If you are handed a gift, accept it gratefully.

Step 11

Continue to have a conversation with your guide. When your guide leaves, exit through the door of the pyramid and walk back down the path. Come back to the present by gently opening your eyes. Take a deep breath and feel the ground beneath you. Make sure that you feel fully present in the room before you move.

Step 12

If you have received a gift, think quietly about the meaning of the gift. If you have received an image, think quietly about the meaning of the image.

Step 13

In your mind's eye, close up each of your chakras from the top down. See the petals of each chakra closing up into a tight, furled bud.

Step 14

To finish and ground yourself, see roots running down from each of your feet deep into the ground.

Using a pendulum to communicate with your spiritual guide

A pendulum is a really simple tool to use. You can use it either to get in touch with your instinct or as a tool to communicate with your spiritual guide. If you do use the pendulum, it is important that you do it from a neutral mindset, because it is easy to influence.

Choose your pendulum carefully. I like to use a metal or crystal pendulum. If you use a crystal one, use one made of quartz not glass and make sure that you clean it with water and salt to remove other people's energies from it.

Hold the pendulum in your hand and ask it to give you a yes. It will either swing horizontally or swing around and around. Ask your pendulum to give you a no. It should give you a different signal. The more you use your pendulum, the better attuned you will be.

To use your pendulum to communicate with your personal guide, start with the intention that you are setting up this relationship.

Hold your pendulum, and ask if your guide is present. It should give you a yes. If it does not, work through the guide meditation (see page 152) before trying again.

Now ask if your guide is willing to communicate with you through the pendulum. If you get a clear yes, you can proceed.

Have a question ready to ask your guide. Start with something simple at first, so that you build the relationship step by step and really get to know your guide. Remember that the pendulum can only give yes or no answers. Please be careful, too, not to anticipate what the answer will be, so that you do not influence the pendulum.

As you use the pendulum regularly, you may feel the presence of your guide energetically coming into the room or space you are in. This might be felt as a temperature change or perhaps a tingling in your arm or neck as the guide makes an energetic connection to your auric body. This is the shadow energy body that surrounds you. If you do not feel anything, that is fine. It does not mean that the guide is not present, but just that you do not tune into energetic changes in that particular way. Store your pendulum in a special box somewhere or even on your altar, where the energies can be kept clean. Please also clean it regularly with water and salt, or using any other form of energetic cleaning you may know, so that it can easily receive the higher vibrations of your guide.

SUMMARY

Work with spiritual helpers, including gods and goddesses, to help you to realize your prosperity intentions. Remember to choose who you want to work with because you are genuinely drawn to their energies. Use your heart, not your head.

Do take the time to make a connection with your own spiritual guide for development. Your guide is always there to help you if you ask, but by forging a strong connection through visualization (see page 152) or the pendulum (see page 155) you will open yourself to receive their messages much more easily.

Developing these relationships will help you to know what to do in times when the path ahead is not clear; you will always have a friend and protector on your side who wants to achieve the best for you in your life.

NOTES

CHAPTER 7

Daydream your future

'DO NOT VALUE MONEY FOR ANY MORE NOR ANY
LESS THAN ITS WORTH; IT IS A GOOD SERVANT
BUT A BAD MASTER.'
ALEXANDRE DUMAS

You can boost your visualization power through regular 'daydreaming', and this chapter will show you how. Any kind of life change can be speeded up by practice on the inner levels of the mind. Daily or regular practice will help you really get to know yourself on every level and also create a clearer channel for communication with the spirit world. You can use any of these visualizations alongside your chosen prosperity rituals.

In this chapter you will learn about:

♣ Finding inner space

♣ Boosting your power of visualization

♣ Exploring your inner self.

Every religious and spiritual practice on the planet teaches some form of meditation or visualization. Monks, priests, nuns, shamans and wise men and women sit quietly or meditate to drumming or music, in order to still the conscious mind. When the conscious mind is stilled, the voice of inner wisdom that comes from the spirit world can be heard more clearly. This chapter will teach you ways of accessing the wisdom of your inner self and spirit. These methods are all visualizations or 'active' meditations.

Quietening the mind

Here is an easy way to begin. You can either sit in a quiet space where you will not be disturbed or put on some calming classical music in the background to change the vibration of your space. Be careful to choose music that does not have words because the words may interfere with the imagery in your mind. You do not need to use the same music each time you meditate. Vary it according to what you feel is right on the day. Different pieces will spark off different images in the mind.

This is a very simple relaxation method. All the other daydreaming methods in this chapter follow from this ability simply to sit, breathe and immediately still the mind. As you become more practised, you will no longer need to use the metaphor of the elevator or the room. Instead, simply close your eyes and go down into this quiet place.

When you relax in this way, your mind goes into 'alpha state': your brainwaves slow down and you are able to access the deeper levels of your unconscious mind. Time passes at a different rate in alpha state so, if you find it easy to drift off, remind yourself before you go into this meditative trance that you will wake up at the signal of the piece of music you have chosen (or another preset signal).

Simple relaxation technique

Sit comfortably with a straight back in an upright chair. Your legs should be uncrossed. This is the ideal position for meditation because it opens up the energy channel of the spine, which can act as a conductor, bringing down higher vibration energies from the spirit world into this world. Close your eyes and take a big, deep breath in through the nose and out through the mouth. Let your body relax. Let your arms rest gently on your lap, and let your legs sink into the floor.

Now take two more deep breaths, once again inhaling through the nose and exhaling through the mouth. As you breathe out, feel any tension just drop out of your body. Say to yourself: 'As I breathe out, all tensions and worries and stresses of the day melt away into the floor below. I am deeply relaxed.'

Feel your eyelids become heavy. If you wish, you can check your eyelids: slowly open them and close them, feeling the relief of being able to close them again and go deeper into sleep – this wonderful state of daytime dreaming meditation.

Now imagine that there is an elevator in front of you. You walk into the elevator and see that there are ten floors. You are currently on the tenth floor. Press the button with '1' on it, so that you can go all the way down. As the elevator descends, each button lights up in turn. You see the numbers flashing in descending order: 10, 9, 8, 7, 6, 5, 4, 3, 2, 1.

When you reach the first (ground) floor, you will see the door to a room in front of you. This is your room of relaxation. There is a bed here. It looks so comfortable. Enter the room, lie down and relax completely.

Remain in this place for five minutes or so at first (or 15 minutes or more if you want to extend the time as you become more practised).

When you want to come out, just get back into the elevator and press the button to the tenth floor. See the numbers going up from one to ten. When you reach the ninth floor, feel the energy beginning to return to your body. As you reach the tenth floor, take a big, deep breath. Open up your eyes, and slowly bring yourself up to conscious awareness, feeling the energy return to your legs and arms, eyes and mouth, head and neck. Feel your breathing come back to normal. Wake up easily, and when you are ready and feel grounded you can get up.

Boosting your visualization power

Visualizations are guided or self-guided methods of imagination and daydreaming. When you visualize, you are asked to see ideas or symbols as you relax. You may also spontaneously become aware of symbols that the inner self and spirit send you as messages. These symbols may not mean anything to you in the moment of meditation; however, after you complete the meditation, you can think about their meanings.

Symbols and their meanings will either be very personal to you – for example, a dog reminds you of the dog you used to own when you were a child and the feelings you had then – or archetypal (a meaning that is common to everyone) – for example, a rose symbolizes love.

HOW DO I KNOW THAT I CAN VISUALIZE?

It is important to say at this point that we can all visualize, although sometimes people will say that they cannot do it. If you think that you might be one of those people, consider this question: What does your bedroom look like? Did you get a picture? See, you *can* visualize.

OK, here's another question to show you that you can not only visualize what is currently in your present, but also what does not yet exist. Go back to that picture that just appeared in your mind and change it. Now imagine getting a big paintbrush. There are three big paint pots in front if you, each in a different colour: red and yellow and green. Imagine dipping the paintbrush into one of those pots of a particular colour and splashing it all over the walls of your bedroom. Now what does that look like? Did you have a picture? If the answer is yes, you can definitely visualize.

Another important thing to remember is that visualization does not just take place within one sense. When you get a visual picture, you can also engage your other senses – touch, taste, smell (and even hearing, in the sense of imagining particularly evocative sounds). The more you do this when you visualize your dreams coming true, the more you will boost the power with which they do so.

Again, it is simple to demonstrate how well you do this already. Close your eyes and imagine that you are holding a lemon in your hand. Bring the lemon up to your lips and take a big bite out of it. Can you imagine the taste of the lemon?

Most of us when we do this screw our faces up a little or feel our mouths going dry because the mind reacts so quickly to the idea of the distinctive acidic taste of the lemon.

How about this? What would it be like if you walked into your kitchen or a restaurant that you know well and you smelled bread baking? Or there was coffee on the stove? How strong were those images for you?

Does your image need a boost when it comes to your sense of smell? Imagine something with a really disgusting smell. How did your body react simply to the words on the page? Did you tense slightly or wrinkle your nose? Then the image is working. Well done.

Next, to touch. What does it feel like to be snuggled up in bed, wrapped up warmly? Did you get a picture with a feeling when you read this question?

What does it feel like to have the sun beating down on you, so that you feel warm all over, bathed in its rays? What does a favourite piece of clothing feel like when you think about it? What does it feel like to hold someone close: a lover, or baby or a pet? What does it feel like to be held in someone else's arms?

How about your feelings? Think very quickly of a time when you felt mildly stressed or uncomfortable in a situation. How quickly do you experience the same feeling? Notice what your body does in response to the image. When we are stressed or feeling any kind of negative emotion, we shrink inward – both on a physical and an auric level.

Now, to feel good again as quickly as possible, think about these situations. Imagine being with a group of people and really finding something funny – you might be listening to a story or joke or watching a show or film. Can you imagine being with someone and being really happy? Can you imagine doing something and feeling very excited?

When you think of any of these situations, notice how quickly your body recovers – which means your vibration lifts very quickly as well. Notice how quickly you can adjust your thoughts – in a matter of seconds. Notice also how easy it was to visualize with feelings attached – which is very important for working with the Law of Attraction (see page 23).

THE IMPORTANCE OF INTENTION

Your intention for a visualization is key to the success of your visualization because thought affects everything we do. As with every ritual, be clear ahead of any visualization *why* you are doing it and *what* outcome you want as a result of doing it.

If you have several different cosmic orders such as a new car, home, new refrigerator etc, you can either visualize yourself having these during one daydream, or you can set up different rituals that relate to the different intentions. Make sure you are clear for each goal why you want it. What you really want on a conscious and unconscious level will be what is manifested.

What can you expect to happen as a result of meditation?

Even though it may seem that you are not doing a great deal by sitting and imagining within your mind, this inner work has immediate effects on your outer reality. This works in a similar way to carrying out any regular ritual such as the ones described in Chapters 4 and 5. Even if you do not think you have experienced a great deal within the visualization, if your intention is clear, you will still see results.

After doing this inner work for a while, you will find clues in your everyday life that your circumstances are changing. You may be offered work or another opportunity to earn or invest money. Or you may spot an opportunity to make a connection that leads you toward one of your prosperity goals.

If, on the other hand, your intentions when you do these visualizations are unclear, you will get unclear results in your life and it is easy to go off your path again. It is really worth spending a few minutes thinking about the major goals that you want to manifest and the changes you want to make *ahead* of each visualization.

Smash through your prosperity blocks

Step 1
Relax by breathing deeply and stilling the mind. Do this technique with or without music. You can use the elevator technique (see page 161) or simply relax by closing your eyes and relaxing your muscles. Breathe deeply to release all the tension.

Step 2
Enter your relaxation room. As you do this, you notice that there is a door that opens outward. Walk through it.

Step 3
Imagine that you are now standing in a garden. Look around the garden, and notice what state it is in. Is the garden already in full bloom or are the seeds yet to blossom? Perhaps there is some weeding needed or it may already be perfectly ordered.

Step 4
Spend five minutes here in the garden noticing what you experience as you explore. This is the garden of your unconscious mind. When you spend time in it, you will get to know yourself better. Enjoy the experience of being here.

Step 5
Now, ahead of you, notice there is a path. Walk along the path until you come to a block of some kind. It may appear in the form of a wall or an object. You cannout move around this block until you get rid of it.

Step 6
Notice on the ground or next to the path that there is an object you can use to smash through the barrier. You can grow to whatever size or strength is needed to wield this tool and smash through the barrier, so that it is totally removed from the path. This barrier is a prosperity block.

Step 7

Once you smash through the barrier, you will see in front of you that the path leads to a body of water. There is a waterfall and a box of treasure within it, symbolizing the flow of prosperity in the universe and the treasure you will take from it. Step into the waterfall and feel yourself showered with the abundance of the universe. Take whatever treasure you like from the box. Imagine that there is so much you can have whatever you want and bring it back with you along the path into the garden.

Step 8

Before you leave the garden, thank the universe for the abundance that it is giving to you now and in the future.

Step 9

Walk back into your room and out through the normal door. If you are using the elevator technique, press the buttons to bring yourself up.

Step 10

Bring yourself back into conscious awareness by taking a few deep breaths to bring yourself up out of this light trance. Next, open your eyes and come back into the room, feeling happy, rich and prosperous, and filled with gratitude for all you have received.

You can repeat this meditation whenever you like. You may well find that your garden changes, giving clues to your state of mind at any one time. Do take note of what you find: whatever it is will be absolutely perfect for where you are right now. Pay attention to the feelings you get when you are in the garden. Your spirit guide will alert you to anything you need to know through feelings, as well as through messages. If you like, adapt the guided visualization in Chapter 6, asking to meet your guide in the garden as a way of receiving messages here.

Goal Booster

To boost your visualization power, use the relaxation method earlier in this chapter to quiet your mind (see page 161). Do this exercise with or without music. Before you begin, decide which of your goals you are going to visualize within the meditation. Again, if it helps, you can enter your relaxation room and take a different door into this new place described below. If you are more practised, simply relax and find yourself immediately in the corridor.

Step 1

Imagine that you are walking down a corridor with one or more doors. This is the corridor to your future. As you walk down the passage, feel how excited you are about the fact that you are about to view this future life. As you come to the right door, open the door handle and walk through into your new life.

Step 2

Now explore every aspect of this new life in as much detail as possible. If you want to change any of it, you can do so by manipulating the pictures. For example, supposing your intention is to manifest the money you need to open a clothing boutique. Imagine that the door takes you straight into the boutique. Walk around the space and notice what it looks like – as if you are a building inspector coming to check that the builders and decorators are doing a good job. You have the power to order anything in here to be changed. Go into every corner. Lift up the products you are selling; smell, examine and feel. If you want to change the wall colour, change it. If you want to expand the size of the retail space, do so. Notice your appearance in the future. Notice what you are feeling. If you want to change anything in your picture, then do it. You can do it in an instant. When you are satisfied with what you see and the way you feel about it, leave the room and shut the door, knowing that everything is in place.

Sometimes, as you do this exercise, your spirit guide will give you a message linked with this future about an opportunity that you need to seize or a step you could take to bring it closer to you. Be alert for messages. These may appear in the form of an image or idea that suddenly comes into your mind or in a figure who appears in the dream and tells you something.

Sometimes, too, you will notice an object that stands out in the daydream and makes an impression on you that you carry back to your waking consciousness. If this happens, be sure to make a note of it and write down all the associations you have with the object or consult a book on dreams and their images/symbols. There are many archetypal images that we share as human beings that have standard interpretations. Other meanings may be personal to you. You will know when you have hit the right interpretation because it will 'feel' right.

If you get a picture of the dish without the flavour – that is, a picture of your goal without any pleasure or joy attached – change the picture.

Take the time to explore each of your dreams in turn. If you do not find it easy to explore these, do the exercise on page 170 to improve your visualization. Always pay attention to your thoughts but also to your feelings. It is the strength of feelings attracted to thoughts that the Law of Attraction really responds to.

Banknote visualization exercise

This is a very simple visualization exercise. You do not even need to go into a meditation or trance state to practise it. Simply close your eyes. Being able to see money in detail in your mind's eye makes it easier to visualize having wealth in your life in the future.

Step 1
Hold a banknote in your hand. With your eyes closed, explore in your mind what it looks like. This is a way of stimulating the visual sense. Imagine your hands holding the note. See its colour, its size and any pictures or patterns on it. Sense in your mind what it feels like to hold the note.

Step 2
Once you have a clear picture of the note in your head, you can begin to manipulate your imagined image.

Step 3
Now see yourself in the picture holding the note. Put it into your purse or wallet, and imagine walking into a store or shop. Take out your purse or wallet, and remove the note. Imagine that you are spending this money in the store. Think about what you are buying with it. Whatever you buy is going to give you great pleasure, so you gain enormous satisfaction from paying for your purchase with the note because you feel happy with what you receive in exchange. Please give yourself the time to feel the positive emotions fill your body as you hand over the note.

The ever-filling wallet

The next stage of the visualization exercise opposite is to imagine that your wallet or purse is always full. However many notes you take out of it, it always remains stuffed full of more notes.

Step 1
Let's imagine a scenario. Put yourself back into the store or a place where you are going to buy something you really want to have in your life. Perhaps it is a big purchase such as a car, for example. Think about what it is going to be before you close your eyes. By the way, it does not have to be an object; it could be an activity or any purchase that contributes to you discovering a way of life that makes you fulfilled and content. This includes paying bills.

Step 2
Now, quiet your mind and take yourself immediately to the scene. You can see whatever the purchase is that you are going to buy. You feel satisfied that by paying for this your life becomes better and better, and it enables other positive choices in your life. Get clear on this in your mind before you proceed.

Step 3
Imagine that you are at the counter or payment point ready to make your purchase. You can see the person you are about to pay. You take out your wallet or pocketbook. As you open it up, you see that it is filled with banknotes. Take out the notes and spend them in your mind. As you take out the notes and hand them over to the seller, notice that your wallet keeps filling up. No matter how much you take out, the amount of money left in your wallet either remains exactly the same or even multiplies. This is because it is your special ever-filling wallet. It will never empty because it is directly linked to the flow of the universe and so will constantly fill whenever necessary.

Step 4
As you see the picture of yourself doing this, be appreciative of the abundance with which the universe is showering you. Enjoy this feeling of wealth and prosperity. Thank the universe for your ever-filling wallet.

Belief booster

This is a guided belief-change meditation that you can use from time to time to help you to really feel the changes that are taking place in your thought processes.

Step 1
Think of a belief that you would like to have. Think about any belief that would lead to a positive boost to your prosperity. If you cannot think of one immediately, write down a belief that you no longer want to have and think about what the opposite belief would be. Think about what kind of opportunities having this belief would attract into your life. Can you imagine how much better your life will be in every way when you adopt this belief?

Step 2
Sit quietly. Close your eyes and take a few deep breaths to still the mind. Let your body relax. Again, you can use the elevator relaxation method and enter your relaxation room (see page 161).

Step 3
Imagine that you are somewhere pleasant and relaxing. This could be outside in nature – on a beach or in a beautiful meadow or wood – or in a beautiful room. In front of you is standing a new you. Look at this new you from a distance.

Step 4
Imagine that, as you watch, you are becoming a very powerful magician. Give yourself a wand or any other magical tool that will enhance your power. You have the power to endow this new you with wonderful qualities and new empowering beliefs that will make the new you into a natural prosperity magnet. You can use this power now.

Step 5
Think about the new prosperity belief that you would like to have. If there is anything you can add to it at this point that will make it an even more powerful thought, do this now.

Step 6

Take your wand or point your finger or use any other magical tool you have at your disposal. You are going to command that belief to drop as a thought form into the energy of the new you, so that all old thought forms that you no longer want are dispersed forever.

Step 7

See the belief dropping into the body of the new you. As this happens, the energy of the thought will start to change the new you. You may see this as a change in the energy field of the new you, or light flooding in.

Step 8

Next, step into the body of the new you, so that you are one person again. Feel the difference in your body in this space as you and the new you integrate. As this is happening and as you are taking on this new belief, start to imagine how differently you will behave. You may notice differences immediately in the way you look at the world around you.

Step 9

See yourself leaping into the future to a time far enough ahead that you can become aware of the changes that have taken place as a result of adopting this new belief. Pay attention to what has changed positively. Are you behaving differently? Do you have different things in your life? What kind of person have you become?

Step 10

Once you have fully absorbed the change in your mind, emotions and body, take a few deep breaths. Open your eyes and come back fully to the room.

Step 11

Finally, with your eyes open, think about how much more powerful you are now. Imagine a future situation and how you will react to it. What has changed? What do you think now?

Energetic visualizations to heal yourself

Practise energetic visualizations to heal any negative beliefs and emotions they produce in relation to prosperity. Carry out the ritual below if you feel any deep negative emotions, including fear, revolving around money.

This technique removes past, negative thought forms from the aura and also helps to stop you from being overly sensitive to group beliefs. If you are a very sensitive, open person, you will pick up other people's beliefs and they will overwhelm your own intuition. On an energetic level this can be seen in the energetic body as thought forms.

You may know that you have an energetic body, as well as a physical body. Within your energetic body there are seven power points known as 'chakras'. These are like battery chargers for the energy body. They need to be kept healthy for your mind, body and spirit to be in balance.

People who possess 'second sight', the ability to see with the third eye, may be able to see negative thought forms within the energetic bodies that surround our physical bodies. Thought forms look like dark patches or clouds within the clear energy of the outer aura. Negative thought forms are sticky, and they attach themselves to our energy when we have strong emotions or hurts from the past that linger in our present.

If you do not have psychic abilities or second sight, you can still practise this visualization, and it will have an effect on your belief system because energy is linked with thought. You just have to hold the intention that, whether or not you can see thought forms in the way that a psychic person can see them, the outcome will be the same.

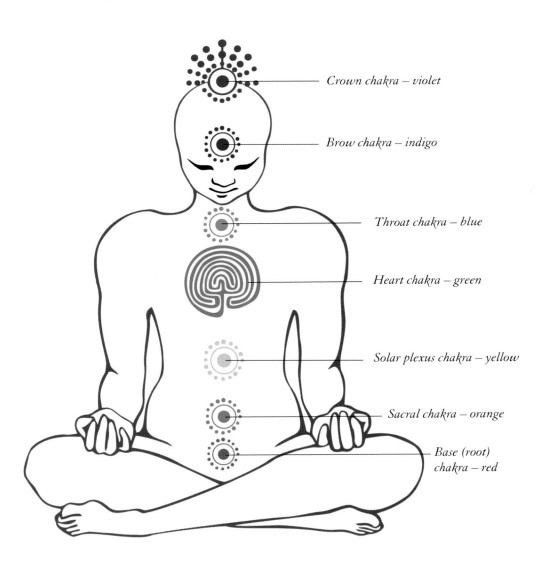

Crown chakra – violet

Brow chakra – indigo

Throat chakra – blue

Heart chakra – green

Solar plexus chakra – yellow

Sacral chakra – orange

Base (root)
chakra – red

Thought-form visualization

The visualization below releases negative or blocking thought forms from the aura. After they have been released, you will feel a sense of lightness, joy, relief or happiness. You can practise this visualization as often as you like.

Step 1
Take at least three deep breaths to quieten your mind. Now visualize your body surrounded by energy. Visualize the seven energy centres, or chakras, within your body (see page 175). Imagine that they are like flowers with petals that can open or shut.

Step 2
Imagine that your crown chakra (the one at the top of your head) is opening up like the petals of a flower to let in the white light of the universe. This white light is love, and love is the most powerful force in the universe. Let it flow through your body and into all of your chakra energy centres. (Another way to visualize this is a large, white net capturing everything in its path.)

Step 3
At the same time, imagine roots growing out of your feet and going deep into the earth, so that you are grounded with the power of the earth as you go through this process.

Step 4
Now imagine that you have a hose running from your solar plexus (the site of the solar plexus chakra, the yellow one in the picture on page 175) out into the earth. If you find any dark patches in your energy field, visualize the white light pushing them out into the earth. The earth is a natural healer. As the dark patches leave your body, the earth will transform their energy and use it to heal.

Step 5
Once every dark patch of energy has left your body, pull the hose back into your solar plexus and close up the energy centre (chakra) once more. Visualize this as a flower closing up its petals.

Step 6

Close each of your chakras in turn in your mind's eye, but keep your crown chakra open just a chink so that light can continue to come in. Do the same with your root, or base, chakra. (See page 175).

Step 7

Keep the roots coming out of your feet into the ground in place, so that you stay connected with the world of matter, as well as the world of spirit, every second of every day.

Step 8

To finish the process, imagine the white light swirling around you, forming a protective net that pushes away any negative energies that try to come into contact with it. Next, in your mind's eye, run a silver-grey cord around you, over the top of your head and under your feet. Let it swirl around your body. You now have a protective energetic seal surrounding you.

Step 9

If you are a very sensitive person who absorbs other people's energies too easily, every morning when you wake you can surround yourself in a white bubble of light. Make sure that the light goes all the way above your head and under your feet, as if you are encased in a big, white bubble bag. This will prevent you from attracting draining or negative energies.

SUMMARY

You now have the basic building blocks by which you can manifest as a reality any change in your life circumstances that you can imagine. If you are experiencing any particular blocks or want to accelerate the changes, use the techniques in this chapter.

By working on your inner world regularly, you will experience immediate and permanent changes in your outer world. Practise your power to visualize. See how easy it becomes to manipulate the images so that you can create future memories – images of yourself in the future.

Explore your inner garden and make it beautiful and ready to receive the prosperous life that you deserve.

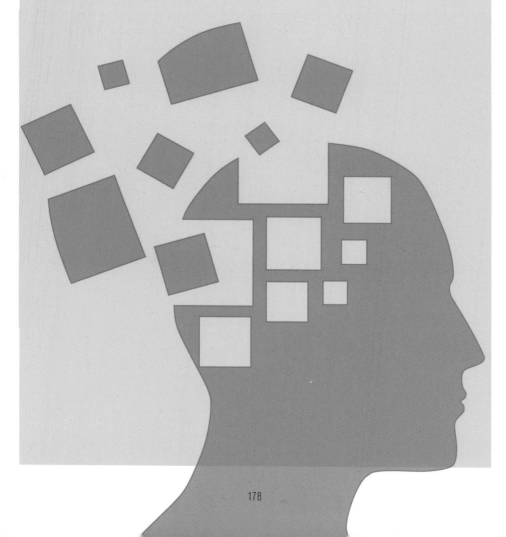

NOTES

CHAPTER 8

Final words

The methods in *The Spiritual Guide to Attracting Prosperity* will ensure that you have a vision of what you want and the kind of life you want to create. They mean you can start to get rid of any inner or outer blocks that are in the way of achieving it. I hope that you will remember that there is no point going after money alone – you are unlikely to get wealth for wealth's sake. The service you give to get that wealth is as important to creating happiness in your life as what you do with this prosperity.

Be bold in your visions of your future and focus on them. You will not know every step of your journey to achieve prosperity by the time you have finished reading this guide. That's absolutely OK. You do not need to. You are only a co-creator of your future. Yes, you must play your part, but the universe will also play its part by bringing you opportunities as you go along. Remember to stay patient. Most people who build great wealth do it over a lifetime – not all in one go. Your life will improve as you journey, regardless of this.

THE ABUNDANT GARDEN OF THE UNIVERSE

Your job is to plant the seeds and water them – make your intentions and take actions toward them.

It is the universe's job to make the seeds grow under the surface of the soil, providing them with all the nutrients they need to sprout above the surface, then blossom into flower. It is then your job to thank the universe for its efforts on your behalf and to admire the flowers. In this way, you ensure that the next time the universe will produce a whole field of blooms for you.

Keep records of your manifestations

Always keep track of your manifestation work. It is important that you can see the results you get from the effort you have put in. Manifestation can be as easy as simply asking for something and receiving it. It can flow very easily as a result of a small change to your beliefs or just by you putting the time into making a prosperity board (see page 119). When it happens that easily, however, sometimes people can become a little dismissive or complacent, and say things like: 'Oh, but that would have happened anyway,' or 'But that was just a coincidence,' or 'Yes, but that can't have been manifestation because it was me who made it happen.'

Yes – that's right. It was you. It did seem like a coincidence. It did happen easily. BUT ... Would it have happened if you had not set your intention years before? Would it have happened if you had not spent time examining your beliefs and passions?

You do not need to be obsessive about your record keeping, but setting aside a nice notebook is a good idea. You can make it into a specific book for your prosperity manifestations, keeping any other manifestations separately, but that is up to you. On the front of the notebook, draw or attach a picture that reminds you of what you are attracting into your life. You can also put your prosperity sigil there if you like (see page 122).

Write down in your notebook what you have done to change your thinking, any rituals you are performing and the list of your intentions. Next, note down what you manifested and when. Pay attention to how near it was to your original intention. You may find that there are times when you get everything you ask for and others when manifestation is a little more blocked.

BLOCKS

There are only a few blocks that can stop your intention manifesting:

♣ Not giving your vision enough time to happen.

♣ Not really believing deep down that it *can* happen.

♣ *Wanting* rather than *expecting*.

♣ Being muddled, confused or ambivalent about what you really want.

♣ Not *feeling* your future can happen.

♣ Not playing your part.

If you feel that you are blocked, examine both your beliefs and your goals. Make sure that you have paid enough attention to making the changes you need to make. The Law of Attraction functions perfectly. If there is a block there is always something YOU need to change.

Your thoughts

Remember that the thoughts you have – both conscious and unconscious, second by second, even if you are not aware of them – are crucial to what will manifest in your life. If you look at most of the millionaires on the planet, they had long-term visions and, even if they came from very tough backgrounds, they did not remain stuck in that mindset because their beliefs were just so compelling. If you still have not overcome any negative conditioning from the past or present, family or peers, please take the time to undo these beliefs. This is not a one-off process. Sometimes we are alerted to old beliefs only by new life experiences. Feed your mind with visions of your future, and take the time to think about what beliefs would support this vision. If it helps, keep looking around for role models who hold these positive beliefs whom you can observe at close quarters or see in the media.

Your emotions

Pay attention to your emotions. These are clues to your thoughts and especially to unconscious beliefs that you may not have put into words. Be clear that your heart and not your head is leading you when you make your vision, otherwise you will not get a future that you truly want. If you feel bad, something is wrong. You have gone off-track in some way. There may be a fear to be dealt with. You may need to make adjustments to your intentions for your future. When you get good feelings going, you will know that you are back on track. Feeling good is designed to be your dominant way of being – it is your birthright to be happy. Being happy connects us to the source – or God and the universe. When you have a clear expectation of receiving your intentions – rather than just wanting or hoping for them –happiness will be your default emotion.

See the opportunities

Make sure that you are picking up on any opportunities and signals that the universe is throwing in your direction to help you to bring your vision to you faster. When you pick up on these signals, act. Remember that our manifestations come about as a result of actions – like the Fool pictured on the Tarot card in Chapter 1 (see page 25). Jump quickly when you are inspired to act and think afterwards. If you know where you are heading, the route is generally clear. If you are not sure what you want to create, you may miss some of these inspired opportunities. If no opportunities appear to be coming your way, go back and check that you really know what kind of future you are seeking to manifest.

Remember that the universe is a universe of abundance, so if an opportunity is missed there will be another. The universe will hear the intentions you have set as a future memory and do *everything* it can to help you realize them. It will bring you opportunity after opportunity for action. This is why, if you have not manifested exactly as you want *yet*, you must nevertheless remember to thank the universe for whatever you receive. This will keep you in the way of abundance thinking. The universe has followed your instructions as precisely as possible for the moment.

Keep records on a quarterly, half-yearly or yearly basis. Review and reward your successes. Notice the changes you can make to become even more effective. Adjust your prosperity board (see page 119) if need be. Add some rituals to your regular practice. Examine your beliefs and how well you know your own thinking.

Sit and meditate on what you have achieved and not achieved. If you have manifested money but not prosperity, take as much time as you need to really let yourself dream. More often than not, the biggest blocks to manifesting are not knowing *what* one wants or not setting aside enough time for it to manifest. Being very specific and clear in your 'whats', in terms of ten or twenty years' time, brings in such a pull of energy from you to the universe it often unravels a lot of belief blocks along the way.

Commit to yourself and your unique vision for your future, and you will reach it and live a rich and fulfilled life.

May you realize all your dreams and transform your life. Be happy and prosperous.

Postscript

Now that you have reached the end of this book my wish for you is that your story has a happy ending as well. Take all the time you need to change your life and make it how you want it to be. Learn through practice how the Law of Attraction can bring prosperity into your life every day. Remember: the Law of Attraction is perfect. Clear your blocks, visualise as specifically and consistently as you can the future you intend to create. Take action towards it.

● Decide what prosperity means for you personally, recognising that it is always more than just money.

● Change the story of your past to a happy one. Look at the beliefs you hold about yourself, your past, money and your future. Begin to change your lack beliefs to abundance beliefs.

● Start now with a fresh sheet of paper and begin to dream the life you want to create.

● Look to the invisible universe and the helpers who live within it to help you realise your dream of a loving future.

● Rely on the Law of Attraction as a perfect means of bringing the future you choose to create into your life. Recognise that thoughts and the feelings attached to them will bring the future you deserve. If you aren't getting the future you want, change your thoughts and feelings about what you deserve.

● Set your intention to co-create your future and show your commitment to the universe by taking action towards what you want every day.

● Change your relationship with money. Learn to enjoy it. Get rid of any fear you have attached to the idea of money. Money is simply a means to an end. It is the medium through which you can create more good feelings in your life.

- If you still aren't achieving your goals, change the timescale. Let go of the date you attached to your goals or push your date forward. A watched kettle seldom boils. By being over-attached to results, you push the outcome you want further away.

- Allow enough time for your future to manifest.

- Remember that you can't see the workings of the universe any more than you can see a seed beginning to grow under the earth. When you think nothing is happening there may be something going on that you need to pay attention to.

- Then if you still aren't getting what you want, change something. Change what you are thinking, doing or seeking to create.

- Notice if you have a really clear and specific picture of your future.

- Notice if your picture is good for you and all around you. Make sure it brings balance into your life by questioning why you really want this.

- When in doubt take different actions towards your new future and see what happens.

- Use ritual to reinforce your intentions for your life.

- Watch the people and circumstances coming into your life. As you life begins to change one of the first clues is in the people and events you attract.

- Pay attention to your night time dreams. If you find it easier, use day-time mediation to seek messages from the spiritual universe.

- Forge a relationship with a spiritual guide and let him or her help you.

When you have done everything then trust. Trust is an abundant thinking pattern. Trust and let go, relying totally on the universe to bring you, if not exactly what you have asked for, definitely a future which is even more to your higher good.

Index

Acknowledgements

Fotalia ahhuwenjun 34 below, 119; Ailin 32-3, 170-1; Ainoa 100-1; Ajay Shrivastava 137; Akio Koizumi 66; Albachiaraa 80-1; Ann Triling 46; Antonio Nunes 18, 107 above; Asim 62; Billybear 54-5; Bluedarkat 105; Bunadruhu 114-5; Caroll138-9; ChaosMaker 148-9; Christine Krahl 154-5; Danimarco 102; Draganm 53; Dragut Vasile Adrian 84-5; Dsgdessert 36-7, 57, 60, 88; Egeneralk 129; Ekler 67; Electra Kay-Smith 111; Eugen 178; Get4net 126; Giniebb 150-1; Greek_usik 6-7; Iadams 96: Ian O'Hanlon 22-3: Ievgen Melamud 141; Isis Ixworth 118: James Thew 8-9; Japonka 183; Kentoh 94-5, 124-5; Kudryashka 52, 68, 70-1 below, 104, 130, 132, 172-3, 180-1, 182, Kusuriuri 67 above; Kwadri 58-9, 128-9; Lina_S 44; Luisa Venturoli 92-3, 112 above; Mahesh Patil 121; Marina Zlochin 156; Mattisa 145; Meraklitasarim 106, 165; Michael Brown 32; Mike Price 134; Mmmg 131; Nataly-Nete 160; NaturesPixel 63; Natutik 116-7; Nidhi Hariani 142-3, 144,162-3; NilsZ 103; Nobilior 97; Nubephoto 70-1 above; Olga Bazanova 49; Olga Rutko 76; Olivier Le Moal 17, 19, 48, 99; Onflying 28-9; Paprika 20; Pavel Konovalov 50-1, 106-7 below, 164-5; Petrol 122-3; PixBox 127; Qeidea 4, 72-5; Rolffimages 82-3; Rosendo 108-9; Ruth Cinigalia 146; Shaun McKinnon 10-11; ShineArt09 109 right, 166-7; Siart 158-9; Stef in BA 112 below; Tadija Savic 86-7; Taily 152-3; Tairygreene 34 above, 35 below; TheSupe87 169; TimurD 21; Tolchik 5, 56; Weimei Ji 38-41, 78 left, 177; Xunantunich 24; Yang MingQi 12-13, 64-5; Zubada 185

Thinkstock Hemera 14-15, 16, 26-7, 30-1, 42-3, 78, 90, 136, 138, 186-7; iStockphoto 140, 175; Photodisc 98

PUBLISHER'S ACKNOWLEDGEMENTS

Commissioning Editor Liz Dean
Editor Jo Wilson
Deputy Art Director Yasia Williams-Leedham
Jacket and Book Design www.gradedesign.com
Cover Illustration Tom Lane
Picture Research Manager Giulia Hetherington
Production Manager Peter Hunt